DROPPI

DROPPING THE P BOMB

EMMA LAWTON

© Emma Lawton, 2016

Published by Emma Lawton

www.droppingthepbomb.com

A CIP catalogue record for this book is available from the British Library.

ISBN 978-0-9935786-0-1

Book layout by Clare Brayshaw

Cover design by Jamie Lawton and Emma Lawton

Prepared and printed by:

York Publishing Services Ltd
64 Hallfield Road
Layerthorpe
York YO31 7ZQ

Tel: 01904 431213

Website: www.yps-publishing.co.uk

Dedicated to the memory of Hardip, Olga and Dipak, who taught me in different ways that life is a spectacular thing and to fight for it to stay like that every day.

About the author

Emma Lawton was born in Bedfordshire in the 80's. She works as a Creative Director in London, runs her own online store, is a market trader, charity campaigner, talk giver and girlfriend when time allows. She never met a sequin she didn't like and her wardrobe is 70% ball gowns. Emma was diagnosed with Parkinson's at the age of 29.

You can follow Emma on Twitter @ems_lawton

Preface

I'm Emma and I have Parkinson's. I just turned 30 which was terrifying enough. And I've moved back in with my parents because I'm buying a house. So I pretty much just need to get married and I'm the full set of answers to a *Cosmo* magazine stress questionnaire.

You're probably frantically Googling Parkinson's as you read this, I know it's what everyone does, to be honest I was Googling the whole way home from the hospital appointment where they told me it was a possibility, throughout the day after my MRI scan and sneakily under the table when I went in for my results and we all knew it was going to be 'interesting news'.

That's why I prefer to drop the P bomb by text or Facebook message, not because I'm scared of talking about it, but because it gives people at least ten minutes solid Googling time, 12:52 if they get distracted by a cat video on YouTube.

Anyway, imagine one of those passing of time montage things and you're back in December 2012. I'm trussed up in a sequin number in a hotel in Norfolk, it's my dad's 60th, the whole family and all his friends are out in force, I've got a gin and tonic in hand and I'm working the room like any good daughter at a social gathering when a family friend floors me with five words.

'What's wrong with your arm?'

She's sussed me. It's game over. I'll now not be able to get away with dodging my doctor's appointment to see if I have carpal tunnel; Mum and Dad have heard her and are giving me knowing looks. Drat. Ten months of trying to ignore the fact that my right arm has a mind of its own are over, I'll have to resign myself to the fact they'll be smug that they knew I should see a doc. Parents One Emma Nil.

Time montage forward a few weeks and I'm at my local surgery, she's nice for a doctor, but she seems to be taking my arm a bit seriously, making me walk up and down the corridor (those are legs, love) and hitting me with the hammer thing that hurts a bit but doesn't make anything move except for my foot which wants to kick her for whacking me. She refers me to the neuro department of my local hospital and I know she has to do that to be cautious so I don't judge her too heavily on the fact I'll have to take another day off work and haul my stupid arm down to the hospital on the bus.

A mini montage later (things move quicker when the NHS are worried) and I'm in the office of a charming neurologist whose soothing voice puts me into the sort of listening coma only normally achieved by a sixth form maths student at last period on a Friday. He seems surprised that I came to see him alone. I seem surprised that he doesn't think a 29 year old can manage six stops on the bus. I slip out of my coma around the point he P bombs me. Very subtly. So I almost miss it. And I realise I probably should have brought an adult with me because 29 isn't old enough to hear that word unsupervised by a hug-providing grown-up. But he's saying it's a possibility not a definite. So he books me for some scans and I leave. And I call my grown-ups. And I Google. And I cry a little bit.

The scanning was interesting. They pretty much just plugged me into some headphones blaring Adele and scanned the living daylights out of me. I had a cold and there was a glass shield over my face to stop me moving and I was willing myself not to sneeze. Or cry. Or dash my brains out on it (Adele can make me go either way). And then we were done and I went back to work. And they told me not to think about Parkinson's. But Google is like a magnet for the concerned and curious and all the old folks with their walking canes and pained faces peering out of my iPhone window at me knew just as well as I did, I had it.

P Day

Phew!

The four letter word you'd least expect to fall out of your mouth the day you get diagnosed with a long term illness. I can think of at least two other p words which would have probably more accurately described the situation. One s word that would have been apt. And although I only allow it on special occasions, the c one might have made an appearance and been excused. My one opportunity to use the c word, AND it be a situation that warrants it, and I say *phew!* Phew!

There's a good reason though. I thought I was going to die.

I've always had a very blasé approach to popping a clog. Kicking the bucket. Pushing up daisies. It's not something I've really thought about in any detail, but being an atheist I think when you're gone you're gone and I've always been ok with that. Live life now and have no regrets. Buy those trainers. Eat that cake. Kiss your work colleague.

I've been fortunate that death hasn't played a big part in my life so far. I still have a grandparent (fingers crossed) and my family and friends are well and happy (touch wood). Death to me has been something that happens to older people when their lives have been filled to the brim and there's room for no more. It's always seemed a bit like Darth Vader (go with me on this). Terrifying from a distance, a wheezing mass with a plastic hat close up.

Undignified. Absurd. Bleak. I've hated the idea of it but it's never scared me.

It's a very different matter when you think it's coming for you, when they're testing for oodles of things that could stop you in your tracks. It suddenly screams into focus that you're just flesh and bone and a whole mess of other crap that you just assume is working as it should. Suddenly every bus that flits past you might run you down. Every chip that passes your lips is going straight to your heart. Every weirdo on the train might lurch at you at a second's notice. It feels like everything is out to get you and it's not. Hundreds of little irrational fears stream through your head every day. You expect jumbo jets to crash through the ceiling while you're watching *Homes Under the Hammer* because nothing is impossible any more. But the one thing you can't think about when you're waiting for scan results is the real and very possible fact that there's something wrong with your brain, because that's too frightening to even consider. So you bury it down and worry about something, anything, everything else instead.

Today's worries are whether the girl I'm staying with will ever get out of the shower, whether my parents will get to London on time, whether the hospital café will have Dad's favourite muffins, whether my jeans are just the right level of rolled up, whether my workload is piling up in the office, whether everyone's going to cry if it's bad news and whether I should have worn waterproof mascara.

So the phew is warranted. Because I'm back in the Consultant's room. And I have my grown-ups with me. And they're saying it's Parkinson's. And I'm not going to die.

P Day + 1

'Trust you to get an old persons' disease'.

I've never been so glad to be teased about something before. I worried that people would stop treating me like me, they'd pussyfoot around, they wouldn't laugh in my company, I'd get that tilty headed pity face, and weirdly those things would be worse than the Parkinson's because then it would mean it's won.

I needn't have worried. Every text I sent got one more positive in return. Or a joke. Or teasing verging on abuse. Or a plan for how we'd fight it as Emma's Army. I think there's not really an option to not be fine. There are worse things to get (like the other C word) and those things are devastating and for a period of time they destroy your life and the lives of those around you. But with something like Parkinson's, it's not short term, it's not life destroying, you can still drink wine, and you make a plan for the long term, how you can get on with being you for the rest of your life. How you can still do nail art. How you can join a band and play drums even though you have no rhythm. How you can wear high heels. How you can dance like a complete idiot. How you can be a bridesmaid at your best friend's wedding. How you can meet someone who loves you shakes and all. How you can have children. Keep your job. Make a home. Grow old disgracefully. And all those things are strangely exciting because you know somehow, with the help of jokes and your Army and copious amounts of Green & Black's, you can beat it.

P Day + 2

I'm back at work and getting back to normality, well as normal as normal can be now. Even on my commute I feel different, like I'm carrying a secret not one of these grey suited, headphone wearing, eye contact avoiding strangers would ever expect. Not only do I have Parkinson's, but, and here's the shocking bit, I'm ok with it. I'm coping. Hell I'm only two days into it but I'm doing well.

Seeing the faces of my colleagues as I walked into the office both broke my heart and glued it back together stronger than it had ever been. They're my 9-5:30 family (9-10:30 if we accidentally end up in the pub) and we've stuck together through thick and thin, bad and good, even the time the café round the corner where we got our bacon sarnies closed down.

And I can feel their support like a summer jumper. You're not sure if you need it yet but it's light enough to not weigh you down. It's good to know it's there in case things take a turn for the worst. It's snugly. And I'm so grateful for it.

P Day + 3

On P-Day my grown-ups asked all the right questions while I sat there phewing. That's why you take grown-ups to things like that. Because they're wise enough to know there's all the time in the world for phewing later. A 30 minute appointment with a neurological Consultant who has just P bombed you is time for questions from me and the grown-ups. Well thought out, possibly even pre-planned, questions.

How quickly will it progress?
How far has stem cell research got?
Is it hereditary?
She was premature, could that be the cause?
I have an early onset degenerative eye condition, could it be linked?
When will she start treatment?
How long has she had it?
What's the next step?
All the while I'm phewing.

I wonder if I'll ever be a grown-up. God no I'm not talking in any morbid long term illness fear for the future sort of way, I'm past that now remember, keep up. I mean maturity wise. Will I ever get to the point where I know the right questions to ask? Where I'm someone's voice of reason? Growing up sounds hard work. I might stick it out as I am.

I remember going on a family holiday at 15 and being at that awkward age where you usually only have time for your friends and boys and have no time for tweezers or your parents. We were swimming in the hotel pool and my dad and I were bobbing around in the deep end and things got... well... unexpectedly deep. Dad tells the story whenever he wants to embarrass me and I swear he hams it up, but apparently I looked him dead in the eye and said 'Dad. I feel different.' Give that man a medal for not laughing. The delivery may have been melodramatic but the sentiment was from the heart, I did feel different to all my friends. While they were racing at breakneck speed towards adulthood, keen to start destroying men's hearts and their own livers, I wanted to stay a child. There was no rebellion from me. I towed the line, I never pushed to go to clubs or not go to school. I was a goody two shoes. A square. If we're being honest I was a bit of a dick. But it boiled down to the simple fact that I loved my parents and didn't want to disappoint them.

I digress. So Dad, willing himself not to crack a smile, sinks his feet to the bottom of the pool and floating over to me says something I'll always remember.

'I'm different too and I don't think I'll ever grow up.'

Sitting in the Consultant's room I felt like a child again and the bit of me that never wants to be an adult is looking at my dad and thanking him for being one for me.

P Day + 4

I usually like being around people. I couldn't be something lonely like a lighthouse keeper or a one man band or an accountant. I love being on my own in small doses, you can potter around, eat bad food and stay up all night. But then slowly I begin to unravel and the freedom of not having anyone check I'm not consuming above the recommended portion of Pringles tips me over into crazy. I like the noise and the warmth of having humans around me, even if I don't know them.

So I'm surprised at the overwhelming feeling washing over me today of wanting to be an island. Unreachable. Remote.

I've had this feeling before though. Something bad happens, I function ok for the first few days then I hit a wall. Like my dad's ancient computer I seem to build up a whole mess of legacy files, scraps of memory and conversations had, snippets of places I've visited and things I've seen, stuff that should have been binned months ago. And then I try and process a big thing and the whole unwieldy inefficient machine crashes. If I stand any chance of moving past it I have to clear my head of all the fragments, switch off and reboot. Back to the black screen, my place of calm. Hover my hand over the power button for just a second and hope that everything will work better this time.

Ok. I'm ready.

I've never really naturally been a high heel sort of girl, I love them in the shop and then I get them home and they return that love by biting my feet to shreds. I've slowly over the years got rid of anything with a heel over four inches so I'm now left with a slightly more sensible selection of wedges, stack heels and feet friendly flats. Pretty ones though, I'm not dressing like a lesbian.

I once dated a guy who thought that girls should always wear heels. How is that fair? While he's running around town in his trainers I'm supposed to be doing the same in vertiginous stilettos that you need a crane to get into? Yeah mate, that's definitely going to happen. He wasn't even offering to buy them for me – that, I could have handled, I could have enjoyed looking at them if they were free, but there was not a cat in hell's chance I was going to spend my hard earned cash on things I'd probably wear once, bleed all over and then relegate to the back of the wardrobe.

At uni, living with mostly boys, I learnt early on that shoes pretty enough to dazzle their way into a club but flat enough not to trip you up when said housemates get into a fight with weapon wielding locals (ok this happened once) and you need to leg it would be my saviour.

So it's sort of nice now to have an excuse not to have to teeter around any more. I can run for buses. I can pull shapes on a dance floor rather than just do the sore shoe shuffle. I don't have to walk down dirty streets with my shoes off at kicking out time. I am sort of classier because of it. Long term illness has its uses.

Today I'm at a friend's wedding. I've got a Grecian gold floor length gown on. And trainers. Victory (and the dance floor) is mine.

P Day + 6

Hangovers. I swear on my liver they get worse as you get older.

When I was a student my world revolved around the drinking of and, when I was sober enough, the selling of, alcohol. I was a terrible barmaid and the green flag by management on drinking during a shift didn't add to my ability to get orders right, give the correct change, and not spill everything everywhere. Every night was party night whichever side of the bar I was standing. Even Sunday wasn't sacred. I befriended the American football team and the day of rest became the day of breast, Hooters, wings and beer tankards as big as your face became the norm. Reefs were strawpedo'd, sambucas slammed and warm flat lager was poured down my throat like they'd just announced the planet's hop reserves were dwindling.

I had a hangover routine. I'd wake up early. Crawl to Tesco to fill my basket with carbs I couldn't stomach and huge bottles of Coke I couldn't carry. Rummage in various handbags for painkillers. Raid every draw in the kitchen for painkillers. Wake up comatose housemates for painkillers. Neck the lot. And then I'd be fine for the day. Sometimes I'd have a power nap before my pub shift but most of the time I'd be fine, buoyed by chocolate and my fear that if I slept I'd miss something fun.

Now, a few glasses of wine and I'm a headachey mess for days. Hangovers become hibernation. Trips to Tesco become the unattainable dream. Whatever that is in the cupboard behind the spaghetti becomes breakfast. If I have a big night out on Saturday I'll still be feeling it come Tuesday.

I can't blame this all on Parkinson's. I have to face facts. I'm just getting older.

P Day + 8

'You have Parkinson's? It must be from doing party drugs, it usually is if you get it young.'

Whhhhhhha?? Chin hits the floor. Eyes squint in disbelief. Legs want to beat a hasty but wobbly retreat out of the door.

Is this doctor seriously suggesting I've brought this on myself? I'm not even seeing him about Parkinson's – what gives him the right to comment? I'm torn between wanting to slap him and throw something witty back but both my arm and my wit have been letting me down a lot recently so I do nothing. I take the prescription and I leave.

And it's only when I get home that I get really angry, like when you're almost in a car accident and it takes about an hour for it to dawn on you what happened and then you can't stop crying. That. And loads of witty things pop into my head. And my hand makes a fist. Oh great thanks guys, bit late though.

P Day + 9

I'm currently living with a friend, my absolute hero, who offered me a room when my living situation changed. It's so much fun, we cook huge meals, watch trash TV and paint our nails more than is probably recommended. We're slowly destroying ourselves with roast potatoes and acetone.

But she has her own life dramas and I can't help but feel I'm not helping her by adding mine to her airspace. So it's crisis meeting with Mum time.

My mum is a powerhouse of problem solving, fixing stuff and cups of tea. Her and my dad have brainstormed and spreadsheeted me respectively out of many a potential crisis and this feels like one in the making so I'm calling in the troops.

We meet in a Starbucks near work and we're not even half way through our caramel lattes and Mum's already got a battle plan together. She'll look for flats to buy, she's freelance and loves being distracted, and I'll move myself back into the family home immediately until I find a new house that's right.

I like this plan for a number of reasons.

a)   *It's the only plan I have.*

b)   *I get to get a house and more importantly buy stuff to go in it.*

c)   *I get to spend time with my family and then they'll see I'm ok and won't worry so much.*

I can't speak for them but I think it must be harder for the parents of someone with Parkinson's than it is for me. I know when I'm feeling ok, because I'm probably in the pub, or having dinner with friends, or buying shoes. They probably think it's hard all the time so the worry never ends.

I think I can solve this by showing them life goes on, by coming home drunk, or full of Chinese food, or clutching bags of trainers. Don't ever say I'm not a giver.

P Day + 10

When I was little I wanted to be an actress. It's all I ever talked about. While putting together our family tree my mum discovered we're descended from circus folk so that makes a lot of sense out of my bolshiness and sequin wearing.

My dad worked for a large car company and they had not one but two amateur dramatic clubs and I insisted on performing with him. I was so small I was only ever a lobster, or a munchkin or part of the chorus but it didn't matter to me, I relished being up on the same stage as my dad. I was always a bit part. But I still loved it.

When I got to the age that I could tie my own shoe ribbons I took classes in ballet, modern and tap and my parents were subjected to hours standing in draughty car parks in Luton watching me not be able to keep up with the other girls in some outdoor dance festival. I was awful. But I still loved it.

Then as soon as I could choose my own lessons at school it was all drama and English lit and language. I even badgered my mum to let me take speech and drama lessons in the evening because I wanted to recite Shakespeare and apparently studying it all day wasn't enough. I took exam after exam until I was a qualified teacher myself and won tons of awards and prizes at competitions. It probably cost a fortune. But I still loved it.

At middle school I took singing lessons to make sure I'd be the full package when I eventually applied to drama colleges. My teacher was a bit creepy. But I still loved it.

As soon as I was finished with my A Levels I started applying at drama institutions. The dream of being an actress was so close. I went to auditions and was told that I was brilliant but that they didn't take candidates straight from school. They needed life experience. That I should come back in a year.

Somewhere during that year I stopped loving it.

And I turned to the only other thing I loved but had sidelined my whole life. Art. Design to be more exact. And I followed in the footsteps of my parents and went into a career in it.

I've always found it strange that after a whole quarter of my life dreaming of and working towards a particular goal it changed in a heartbeat and I didn't fight for it. I just moved on to something else.

But now it makes sense. I'm a firm believer in things happening for a reason and all that other mumbo jumbo. I would have struggled to continue to act with Parkinson's, but it couldn't have been a lasting career. It relies so heavily on being physical and having a loud, clear voice, both of which are now failing me a bit. As a designer I can take my time and get others to help; I can even be in my own little bubble if I'm having the sort of day when I need to be alone. I wonder if my brain knew this.

I took a different path that my ten year old self wouldn't understand. But I still love it.

P Day + 12

I've never been that good with money. But now more than ever, when I'm thinking about getting a mortgage, I need to try and do better. My weaknesses are clothes, shoes and not budgeting. It's been like that for as long as I can remember.

When I finished school, before I went off to university, I took a gap year to cement the direction I wanted to go in. I didn't do the usual middle class thing and go travelling and build mud huts in Nicaragua or an orphanage in Tibet. I got a job as a buyer's assistant in a fashion company and it was brilliant. Still pretty middle class, yeah, I know. I spent my days measuring and fitting garments, learning the design and manufacturing processes and creating mood boards for the new season. I'd waste hours sitting with the print designer who painted everything by hand or hanging around on the top floor where there was a factory where the patterns were cut. It made me sure that design was what I wanted to build my life around. And clothes were what I wanted to spend my money on.

Every month there were big sales selling off all the samples of shoes and clothes that had been bought by the designers to inspire their ranges. I went crazy at these. I was spot on sample size (clothes 12 shoes 7) so I was like a kid in a candy shop grabbing bundles of coats, dresses and bags. Every six months we'd drive out to our sister company's sales where a black bin bag cost a tenner and you could fill it to the brim with clothes. At the time it seemed so important to grab that denim dress or the gold pumps or the mohair cardigan before someone else did, and I think it held me in good stead for future T K Maxx trips, but when I got home 80 per cent would have bits cut from them, sport broken zips or just be hideous beyond belief. So into the bin they'd go. I look back now and cringe at the waste and the polyester.

It set me up badly. Fashion was throwaway. Money was for treating yourself. Bills were paid by grown-ups. Even now I struggle to prioritise things I need against things I want. I have to set up to settle my bills as soon as I get paid or there'd be no money left for them. I don't have the best credit score and my debt doesn't feel like real money so it's all a bit unhealthy and unbalanced.

I think I'm panicking all the more because I'm pretty sure I'll have to stop working full time at some point and having some sort of financial buffer would make me feel better. I've got myself into some bad habits that are going to be difficult to break. Just like this ice block in which I've frozen my credit cards.

P Day + 15

As a designer I am most happy when wielding a marker pen over a blank piece of paper. Better still if there's multiple pens and they're *eek* rainbow colours. A lot of people are scared of blank paper, they think there's an expectation that they need to do something perfect, that you'll spoil the paper if you do something wrong. My view's always been that blank paper is sad and even the worst scribble or daub helps it fulfil its artistic destiny.

Since the Parkies kicked in I've noticed my writing getting smaller and smaller, all twisty and wiry and illegible, apparently this is normal, so I've been fighting back by only ever writing with a huge black pen on massive paper. Shopping lists become epics. Post-it notes fit a word at a time. Birthday cards are frankly mental.

I thought I'd found a way of doing my job; sketches would be a doddle (if slightly oversized) and I could distract from non-straight lines with flashes of colour and shadows of tonal greys and keep detail to a minimum (people don't need faces, right?). But oh no, I have a new nemesis. The white board. There is something about the angle of a white board that my hand won't go in for: it rears up like a dog at a graveyard and won't go any further.

Sadly I found this out in the middle of a client meeting where I was in charge of the sketching, when I drew a car that looked like a turtle, a woman with arms coming out of her hair, a house with no door and was forced to make the international sound for *rescue me* to my colleague. Not only am I the girl who can't draw, I'm now the girl who makes owl noises.

Super.

Mum the freelance procrastinator has miracle of miracles found me a possible flat. One that I like, to be more precise. It's a new build so I'm surprised that I like it, but it's right by the river so I think that might have swayed me.

The only thing is I'm now madly in love with it, all my future hopes are pinned on it, my independence, my happiness, my opportunity to make lots and lots of cushions – but 2,000 people have applied for just 35 apartments. Crap.

Ever positive though I find myself today sitting in the office of a mortgage salesman at a high street bank that shall remain nameless, trying to come across as a sensible grown-up while dressed as... well, frankly, a fairy princess. I possibly misjudged my white floaty dress with the gold spots. Power suit next time.

It's amazing how much they want to know. We're going back as far as when I was a twinkle in my dad's eye pretty much and I'm frantically searching out lost internet banking logins, trawling through paperwork and hoping upon hope that they think I'm a safe bet.

My cushion making depends on it.

P Day + 24

I can imagine the lifeguard at my local pool has seen her fair share of sights. Heavy petting, weeing children, full scale marital domestics. I'm guessing today might have been the first day she saw someone actually try and swim using just one arm and one leg.

My right knee's been a bit sore, something to do with the ligament apparently, so I thought I'd give it a bit of gentle exercise to try and free it up. It had other ideas. I was determined to power through so me and the left side of my body went for a swim while the right side stiffened up like a dead weight. At school we did life saving classes where we had to swim in our heavy clothes so I channelled me circa 1992 and dragged myself to the edge of the pool. I'm completely puffed out, red in the face, gasping like a 40 a day smoker. And I've done one sodding length.

I should be good at this, my family has swimming pedigree. Somewhere in our family tree there's a chap named Jim who was the very first (and possibly last – it doesn't sound like a lucrative career) Professor of Swimming and introduced the crawl into the UK from America.

It's in my genes.

Jim would be disappointed.

Jim can take his crawl and bugger off.

The pool isn't even that deep, I could have probably walked it quicker.

Every cloud has a silver lining. *Silver?* Pah. My Parkinson's cloud's got a sequin encrusted pewter silk hand stitched interior. And that's the fact that I get to spend more time with my family.

We've always been a close bunch, there's not many of us (just me, my mum, my dad, my brother, my brother's girlfriend and their dog) so we talk a lot, we're definitely all oversharers and even when we're all not living under the same roof we know what the others are up to. But there's nothing quite like getting us all in the same room and that's been happening a lot more since I got diagnosed.

I've noticed changes in all of us since we got the news.

My brother seems to have become older than me overnight, its now like I'm his little sis (in height as well as age) and he looks after me whenever I don't fight him on it. He's like a duck, all calm and casual on the surface, legs going mental under the water, he's a huge worrier. We've always been close, never really fought or got on each other's nerves (except for when he was about four and had the most infuriating little bowl haircut and he'd hog the screen when my dad was videoing me playing my recorder) and I think year on year we understand each other more.

My dad wants to mend me, and I know it breaks his heart that he can't. He's always been able to fix everything for me since I was tiny, my dolls house when I was a bit rough with the door, my shelves when I moved into my old flat, my business when I was struggling to make the figures work. But this is a biggie and not even the strongest epoxy resin or neatest spreadsheet can sort this one out. So I guess it's pretty lucky that Dad is also the universe's best supplier of hugs, man they're good. More soothing than a cuppa with two sugars they've got me through some tough times and this is no exception.

My mum has gone into battle mode. She's organised, efficient, knows all the questions to ask and who to ask them to, she's the strongest woman I know. She works in the learning disability sector so she's always been good in a crisis and I know when I'm not around she gets sad about the situation but she never shows it because she knows I need her to be strong so that I don't buckle too. I want to get to the stage where she feels she can tell me when's she's had a bad day or is generally pissed off like she used to.

It's tough for everyone.

But the times we're all sat around the table, teasing my dad for eating two slices of cheesecake (he's where I get the eating from), stopping the dog licking our knees, laughing at Mum for getting tipsy on Prosecco, discussing flooring for my brother and his girlfriend's new house, then we're in our happy place, and Parkinson's can't even come close to touching that.

I'm actually sitting outside. In the sun.

This could be very detrimental to the Kristen Stewart in *Twilight* (or for that matter Kristen Stewart in anything) look I've been sporting recently. Pale skin. Sullen face. Bitch stare.

I've become a bit of a hermit at the weekends since I now live at my parents in the sticks and only venture into London during the week because it's frowned upon to not show up at work. When I was a teenager living here I moaned like a braking bus about the lack of transport to the nearest town where my school was and all my friends lived. I felt like I had to plan everything in advance. That I missed out on all the fun. Those simple trips became expeditions. I was a whiny little shit. There was a perfectly decent bus service every hour from the end of my road.

Now being back I realise I have everything I need here. A garden I can sit in. A full fridge. A comfy mattress and snugly duvet. Unnecessary items that only real grown-ups have in their cupboards like ironing water, boot polish and quinoa. And of course my parents.

I have everything except my stuff. My clothes and belongings are still in London ready to be liberated when I find a flat and have somewhere to put them. It seemed daft to move everything to my parents' house just to move it back again so it's in suitcases and boxes in various flats across London. From Peckham to Archway to Essex there are very few boroughs without some of my stuff in residence. And it feels weird. Like I'm scattered. I'm left with a bunch of clothes that look like I grabbed them in a hurry with no thought to whether they matched or were actually mine. I've got shoes that are missing their pair. I've got three pairs of pants and five socks. I've got a floor length beaded prom dress for some inexplicable reason. Everything I plan to wear or use is somewhere else. It's been more frequent than I'd like that on popping round to a friend's house I've yelled 'Ooh there's my bra'.

But I'm playing the long game; soon I'll have somewhere that's mine and filled with all the things and people I love. Until then I'll just be the bra-less girl who wore a prom dress to work.

P Day + 29

Refresh.

Save 20 per cent on our new summer range.

Refresh.

Your April/May itemised phone bill is now ready.

Refresh.

Refresh.

Refresh.

I'm slowly driving myself mad.

Waiting to find out if you can have the flat you want makes time stand still.

Refresh.

They've said they'll let us know by email so I'm sat at work with my phone glued to my hand and my index finger pressing refresh like one of those irritating bird things.

Refresh.

I was told it would be today and it's 2:31 and I've still not heard anything. Maybe that's bad news. Maybe they just couldn't face letting the unlucky 1,965 people know, hell that's a lot of bad news to deliver in one day, that person deserves cake.

Refresh.

Trying to maintain a level of concentration on the website I'm supposed to be designing is tricky when there's...

Refresh.

Were you happy with your eBay purchase of 100 tea lights? Please leave feedback.

Refresh.

Maybe I'll send them an email chasing. Maybe if they haven't made a decision yet they'll see how keen and polite I am and that'll swing it.

Great.

Dear Daniel, I was just wondering if there was any news on the flats as you said you'd let us...

Screw this.

Refresh.

Oh my god there's an email. From them. Shit. I think I'm having a heart attack. That's not great because then who's going to live in my new flat? Don't jinx it! You've jinxed it now you idiot. Ok breathe breathe calm you're on a sunny beach listening to the waves lap the sand swish swish swish. Ok we can do this.

Ok.

Good afternoon Emma, I am very pleased to formally offer the above property to you. Please find attached a copy of our formal offer letter blah blah blah hard copy blah blah in tonight's post.

Oh.

My.

God.

I got it. Number 51. The beautiful one with the balcony. My first choice. This is bonkers. They picked me.

Hi Daniel, that's great news! Thanks, Emma

That's right play it cool. He doesn't need to know you're sat at your desk with tears streaming down your face and that his email might have just exploded your heart.

P Day + 30

I'm allowed to use the facilities at a client's leisure club. I spend three minutes swimming lengths and 57 minutes in the sauna/steam room/jacuzzi. Why I was chosen to work on a sports related website continues to be a mystery to me.

P Day + 33

Reunions are strange things.

If you've just got married or dropped a sprog that doesn't look like an alien then it's a pretty good excuse to show off. If you've just got Parkinson's, moved back in with your parents, are single and have developed a spot that's starting to resemble a second face the prospect seems a little more grim.

Saying this I was genuinely planning on going today, my old school friends are great and I could have fake smiled my way through it and dodged any tricky questions like a pro, but recently I've been struggling with a tiredness that sleep just can't touch and it won.

It's not like I was particularly sporty or co-ordinated at school, I dabbled in rowing (it meant we were always late back for chemistry) and swimming (firemen came to our pool to train, enough said) so the girls wouldn't look at me and think *Something's wrong, Emma isn't juggling her cutlery as deftly as she normally would.* I'd feel deceitful not telling them somehow. Or like I'm ashamed of it, which I'm not. And I guess I just haven't worked out how to tell people I haven't seen in a while about it in person yet.

Plus babies terrify me.

P Day + 38

Up until now I've been guessing what my flat looks like. I've seen a show flat and a floor plan and merged the two together in my head to guess what it might be like, hardly ideal but it's the only option.

Today, having already said I'd have the flat, I get to see it. I hope it's not got anything weird, that it's not the house equivalent of the gorgeous boy you take home who turns out to have 11 toes.

We put on wellies and visi jackets and hard hats as the place is still a building site and take the lift up. And it's gorgeous. Light and bright, with oak floors and a long balcony the width of the flat. And a cupboard probably meant for hoovers and mops and cleaning products that I've got earmarked for trainers. And a larder probably meant for canned goods and condiments and root veg that I've got planned for gin.

I'd describe myself as the indoorsy type. The grass makes my skin itchy. The ground hurts my bum in a way that even copious blankets can't remedy. Being out in the air makes me scream inwardly *I'm melting! I'm melting!* I have no idea where this comes from. My parents permanently have a healthy glow and like nothing better than farting around in the garden. I'm happier hibernating indoors. I reckon if I didn't have a job I'd never leave the house. My vitamin D levels rely on me being gainfully employed.

Sadly other people seem to like sitting on nettles and being bothered by enthusiastic dogs so I find myself at a picnic trying to look breezy about it because, and don't laugh at me, I like a boy and he seems to be ok with that kind of thing. We'd need to work on that if this is going to have any kind of future.

He's beautiful. All dark eyed and brooding with a range of facial expressions that make Lee Evans look like a stiff. That's high up in my man criteria, I like expression full faces. Even better if the eyebrows get involved. And he's kind and makes me feel giggly and girlie and like my heads got bubbles in it. And best of all he knows I have Parkinson's and still gives me the look that makes my stomach jump and my ovaries wiggle with expectancy. God we'd have cute babies.

Snap out of it girl. All his friends are here. They're the vetting process to get to the next level. Laugh. Eat the mini sausages. Compliment the girl ones on their hair/dresses/ability to sit on grass without going rashy. The girl ones are easier to win round. Winning boys over requires sport knowledge.

He's dreamy. He's got that whole manly vibe going on that makes me want to swoon like a Victorian chambermaid. Those eyes. The dark hair. The...

THWAK!

Jesus christ mother fucking fuck what the hell was that? I have a searing pain running down my jaw and I'm still smiling. Give that girl an Oscar. *And the best actress in what the fucking shit arse just happened goes to Emma.*

One of his friends just threw a ball, I want to say AT me, but TO me is probably fairer. To my right hand. And right hand says no to sports. Right hand likes to idly sit by while face, all gallant, steps up to make the catch.

Ouch.

But he's still smiling at me. And my heart's like butter. And it doesn't matter that I'll probably need facial reconstructive surgery to even out the ball shape in my cheek because he seems to be the kind of boy that would look at me like I'm a rare and exotic bird even if I'm more of a pigeon.

We like that kind of boy.

P Day + 44

Today almost went down in history as the first time someone has actually died of embarrassment. I went to see my new specialist with my parents and the nurse starts to list out the possible complications of the meds they're planning to start me on: the usual; sickness, dizziness, sleepiness, near death, addiction... oooh this is getting good tell me more... gambling, shopping (nurse flicks her eyes at my new Nike concealed wedge high tops), food, sex... Oh cringe. Did she seriously just say that? *With my grown-ups here? They might not have heard. Quick, make a joke about trainers.*

As a family we've never been big on discussing the s word. And I'm fine with that. I don't think I've grown up any less aware, I'm just probably a whole lot less mentally scarred than my friends whose parents gave them blow by blow accounts. I've just weirded myself out even writing that sentence. I learnt about carnal knowledge from a robot on a school PSE video. There was a little confusion that needed straightening out between me and my mum about whether it was just robots that had sex but once that was clear I knew enough to find it all hilarious. The school made the error of making our sex ed day the same day we started reading *Macbeth* in English class. Lady M's heartfelt *unsex me here* speech got far more giggles than it should have resulting in the entire class being sent to see the headmistress.

I went to an all girls school so boys weren't even something that crossed our minds until our GCSE year, apart from one particularly ahead of the game girl who got started early and filled in all the blanks in our knowledge. Thanks to her and a robot I was educated enough to stop my parents having to give me the formal chat.

Nowadays, it's the thing that goes unspoken, I'm sure they know it happens but there's a big difference between that and thinking your daughter might turn into a sexual deviant.

Writing a boy into your book is more terrifying than introducing them to your parents. Once they're in they're in and can't be unwritten. Parents can forget.

I'm considering adding one to my story, not because I need a Prince Charming to ride in on his mighty steed but because I want one. This damsel can save herself but wouldn't complain at being rescued from time to time.

But there's a biggie that's worrying me and that's why it all feels a little bit more Brothers Grimm than Disney right now. I'm not sure if my story has a happy ending yet so it's difficult to know whether it's fair to bring someone else along for the ride. He knows what I'm dealing with but I don't know if he knows what it'll mean for him, that my lows might be huge, my challenges terrifying, and that he'll go through all this with me. That one day I might not be able to hug him without it feeling angular. That I could make stupid decisions. I feel like I want to sit him down and tell him, so it's all laid out but I'm frightened that he'll run, there's a part of me that thinks that I might if the tables were turned. It's just so early to be talking like this, we're so new, but if I wait and never ask him if he's sure it could take years, when we've built a life together, for him to realise that he's not.

I'm taking time out and going to my parents' caravan by the sea for the weekend to torment myself with this in different surroundings. I want to talk to them about it but I stop myself because it's bad enough that Parkinson's is sneaking into my head when I should be excited, without it getting into theirs as well. So we eat fish and chips out of paper and walk for miles beside the sea and we rummage for treasures in antique shops and lick hot chocolate foam off our lips. Until I know I'm ready to ask him whether he wants to be a character in my book long term. If he knows what that could mean.

And he says yes.

My friend Kev and I have been through some scrapes. There was the time we lost each other in a gay club and he found me sobbing at the feet of a Drag Queen as she sang *It's Raining Men*. There was that incident with the coffee percolator that taught both of us to never push down that hard again. There was a story involving poo we vowed never to speak of again but that we proudly recount at every social gathering. We've eaten salad in bed on a Saturday night because we're too lazy to go out. We've seen musicians/accountants/stationery men come and go in each other's lives. We've successfully never managed to both live in London at the same time. He is my partner in crime. And I'm so worried as to how he'll take the Parkinson's.

This is the biggest scrape we'll ever go through. This can't be undone with a cooked breakfast and debrief. It won't disappear in a puff of smoke and a shimmer of sequins like that Drag Queen in Camden. It can't be told to fuck off like the people who crashed the house party who we all thought were someone else's friends. This scrape is for life. And I need a battle plan.

Kev shoots down Parkinson's and my worries immediately. I tell him I think I can cope with it and he replies *So it's Parkinson's with a little p* and the name sticks. Things with a capital always seem more terrifying. Giving a name to something gives it power. Just like Voldemort.

Screw you little p. And your bigger brother.

P Day + 56

I am stupidly competitive.

Not at the normal things, but if there was competitive crafting or web design or homeware buying I'd be front of the queue to sign up. And I'd kick all their arses.

When we were kids we'd go on holiday with my friend Lucy and her family who were all super sporty. My dad invented this water Olympics game which involved us hurling ourselves into the pool to catch balls, swimming lengths astride a giant crocodile and running around the patio with wet feet in what can only be described as a recipe for brain injury. All standard Olympic activities really. My mum couldn't swim, my dad was umpire and my brother was tiny so I seemed to do everyone's races. And boy did I give it some, but usually came in last. Against myself.

Appointments with my new speech therapist and physiotherapist turned into me competing with myself to see how quick I could run, how fast I could drink water, how high and low I could sing (Des'ree eat your heart out), how long I could hold a note. I flippin' won though. Emma of five minutes ago can eat my dust.

Applying for a mortgage might just be the most terrifying thing I've ever done. I have less than a week until I need to be ready to complete on the flat and the big high street bank I've been with for 12 years has just told me (after countless meetings, thorough trawling of my financial history, pretty much assessing every pair of shoes, every lipstick, every nail varnish I've ever bought) that I've been declined.

Err, I'm sorry... what?

And this is via a voicemail. At 6pm on a Friday. And the guy who's been dealing with my application has gone on holiday for a week. And no one can tell me why I've been declined.

I spend too much on clothes?
Used to live with a guy who bought a lot on credit?
Don't have any bills in my name for my last address?
My old landlady used to apply for credit cards to our address?
I'm too young?
I'm too old?
Was it because I wore a sparkly dress to that meeting?
Did I fill in the form wrong?
Do they know I have Parkinson's?
Do they think I'll have to stop working and won't be able to pay my mortgage?

I'm freaking out. I'm sat on a train calling my mum and I'm crying, in front of a carriage of commuters, and I don't even care. In one voicemail they've single-handedly destroyed my future and left me not knowing how it can be fixed.

Mum meets me in the car and I cry the whole way home because I don't know what to do. Because they've left me unsure of why I've been declined I don't know what my next move should be. And when I get home I do the thing they say you shouldn't do and I apply for every mortgage with every company I can find on the internet. Because this is my future and I'm fighting for it.

I'm not normally a fan of waiting. I'm the girl who tuts in that passive aggressive way at the train delay announcement. The girl who pulls a face at the hospital receptionist who says I'll be seen soon. The girl who is one more long toilet queue away from starting to use the *I have Parkinson's card* to jump them.

But delays to the build of my new flat have proven to be a bit of a godsend. What with the small issue of me not actually having a mortgage to pay for it yet. I'm heartbroken and terrified. Last night's scattergun mortgage applying binge has left me with a dent in both my pride and credit file and I don't know what to do. I guess it's a waiting game for now and a nightly prayer to the god of building things that there'll still be a shortage of bricks tomorrow.

Mum is the eternal optimist and for this reason we're going to look at sofas today. An excellent exercise in tormenting myself but one that if I get those teensie tiny flat logistics sorted will mean I'll have something to sit on. And if I don't, well then my parents' garage will become a whole lot more plush.

I've never had a sociable flat before, one that I'm proud to invite people round to, where there's space for anyone other than myself to lounge, where people can move around without bumping into stuff. There was the old fashioned one in the middle of nowhere. The one that I hid from friends because of the various bodged DIY attempts. The one that was pushing the boundaries of how small is too small. The one I only had a room in. They've all been tiny and angular and borrowed. Perfectly nice as far as flats go. But I'm ready to make myself a home.

And a sofa for me is the heart of a home. Where plans are made. Naps are taken. Hugs are given. TV dinners are eaten. Unexpected overnight guests are accommodated. It needs to be a good one. I want the lounge to be 90 per cent sofa, ten per cent actual useful space. And here in front of me there's a beaut, an L-shaped slate grey soft cord-covered one with a comfy pull-out bed. It's perfect.

I find a bed frame and mattress too. It's all going well. Until I remember that the home I'm making isn't mine yet and may never be. But I hug a cushion close to my chest and tell the sofa I'll be back for it soon. And you can't break a promise to an inanimate object, that's the rules.

Independence Day.

The irony isn't lost on me that today was the day I was supposed to be regaining mine and exchanging contracts on the new flat. I still have no takers on the mortgage front and there's still a shortage of bricks so as long as myself and the developers are both in the same state of non-readiness it'll be ok.

It's hard living with your parents when you've just been told you've got something that in the future might limit you. It's like a ticking time bomb until you lose your freedom to do stuff without help and every day counts, the last thing you want is to feel like a child. Don't get me wrong, I'm loving spending this much time with them but I need to start living with the new situation I've been handed and that's difficult when you're protected in the cozy, safe bubble of the family home. Everything's easy there. I need to be out in the wild and know I can cope.

I've always been a bit of a home body, a goody two shoes. Not wanting to upset anyone or disrespect my parents I went through my teenage years worrying about my actions and the effect of them. I once said something out of line and I can still as plain as day remember the look on my mum's face and how I never wanted to see it there again. To this day I fret and run over in my head every little dig or snap I make, every joke taken that bit too far, every sneer my mouth breaks into. Because I want so badly to be a good daughter. And a good person. Because of all the work my parents have done since I was born to take that tiny thing and not break it, always do right for it, put it first. I don't want to waste what they worked hard to cultivate.

But I'm worried that I'm doing too ok with this big life changing news. That the penny hasn't dropped yet. That at some point I'll crack. Their daughter who never steps out of line might really lose her shit. And I don't want them to see that.

I have a habit of borrowing other people's friends.

In my troupe I have a whole mess of stragglers, brilliant people too good to meet once and then forget, friends of friends, friends of colleagues and in some cases friends of people I met through another friend for five minutes in a pub. I'm an avid collector of characters, like my life is a plotline I'm afraid will get stale.

My friends don't seem to mind lending to me. I always look after them and don't lose them. As long as they don't start liking me more than them we're good.

Tonight I'm seeing two of my most recent acquisitions and their lender, Lucy. We've been friends since birth and she's the closest thing I have to a sister, we're like chalk and cheese but it somehow just works. She's getting married next year and did our friendship a huge solid by picking me as a bridesmaid. *Eeeeeeeeeeeeeeeeeeeep* I'm too excited. I haven't been one of those since I was little and they stuck me in a navy sailor dress. I rocked it. Obviously.

The other two are also bridesmaids who I knew a little bit when I was growing up from discos and sleepovers and birthday parties but never spent enough time with them for us to bond properly. As a four we're like some *Sex and the City* cliché of mismatches. There's the foxy blonde teacher with a heart of gold. There's the petite brunette who works in finance and is fiercely loyal to her friends. There's the cool graphic designer with the quick wit and the undercut. And there's me, the shaky one. Slap us down in the middle of Manhattan with some Cosmo's and we're HBO ready.

We've been hanging out a lot recently to plan wedding stuff (ok ok to drink rosé and gossip and probably spend about five minutes doing any quality thinking) and I'm loving having them in my world. I'm at ease with them. I feel like I've known them a lifetime.

And now I have to P bomb them.

Ugh.

Lucy already knows but I feel like I should tell the other girls now we're a collective. Since I was diagnosed the question I get asked again and again is whether I care what strangers think when they see me shaking. I genuinely don't worry about that. It's harder to see the look on the face of someone who cares about you when you tell them your brain's not working properly.

I wait until we've all got a glass of rosé in our hands because there's nothing more important than vino. And then I hurl it like a grenade into the conversation. And I watch their faces drop for the quickest flicker of a second, the worry and the unfairness of it all runs like a shadow across their expressions and then it's gone, replaced by steely determination and unending support. And I know in that instant they're a long term rental in the world of friendship real estate.

P Day + 69

Reading through all my house buying documentation (planning permission, land registry docs, plans etc) and I've already stumbled across references to rare birds, archaeological finds and having to take out insurance in case I have to repair a church or something. London you're a whole special kind of weird.

Never has life changing news been delivered more casually.

'That's all gone through Miss Lawton.'

Stunned silence from my end of the phone.

'I'm sorry, what has?'

'Your mortgage approval.'

Someone pick me up off the floor.

I didn't even realise she was running a check on me, she probably said it and I was panicking so much my ears closed up. I'd only called this bank on the off chance and because it was pretty much the only other place I hadn't spammed with application forms yet. Weeks of filling in paperwork, online applications and apologetic phone calls to other banks and this woman's just approved me in five minutes. Over the phone. I didn't even have to bring out my power suit.

I think I'm quiet for too long because she asks if I'm ok and a bunch of words spill out of my mouth which obviously sound like *yes* because she carries on reading from her screen about the next steps. And I don't even care what they are, they could be *Deliver six months' payslips to our office on the back of a hungry adult male lion within two days* and I'd manage it.

She says goodbye and hangs up and I hold the phone to my ear for what feels like an hour. I'm tempted to call back and check she said what I think she said but I'm worried they'll reconsider based on the crazed tone in my voice and the fact I'm struggling to get words out in any sensible order. In my limited knowledge of mortgage approvals crazy doesn't earn you a whole lot of ticks.

P Day + 80

I have a work presentation tomorrow and I'm worried I'll shake. I hate the fact I can go in there, uber confident, prepped to the hilt, calm as you like, and one shaky hand can make them think I'm too scared to be up to the job.

So I've just done the obvious thing that any normal sensible human being would do and bought some stilettos in Parkinson's blue. Fix everything with shoes. Little p, I will trounce you.

P Day + 81

The shoes hurt.

Nailed the presentation though. And the woman commented on said foot hating shoes, she can have them if she likes them so much. That'll teach me to buy £5 sale shoes to make a medical statement. Next time I want to stick two (blistered and mangled) toes up at Parkinson's perhaps I should err more towards Jimmy Choos.

P Day + 88

I hit the big 3-0. I've woken up a year older and I'm not thrilled about it. I'm physically exactly the same. My face looks identical to the one I had yesterday. So why is this such a big deal?

Five years ago I set myself a ridiculously unachievable list of 30 things to do before I turned 30, just a bit of fun, 30 things I'd always fancied doing scrawled casually in the back of a notebook.

1. Buy a house (damn it)
2. Be settled with a man (five dates counts as settled, right?)
3. Own my own shop (selling what exactly?)
4. See the Northern Lights
5. Have tea at The Ritz
6. Appear on TV
7. Play in a band on stage
8. Go in a hot air balloon
9. Swim with dolphins
10. Write a published article (I win. I'm writing a whole book [*sticks out tongue*])
11. Visit Niagara Falls
12. Fly in a helicopter
13. Learn how to drum (I can just about do a Meg White, does that count?)

14. Get to 1,000 followers on Twitter
15. Win a design award
16. Win any award (I can see desperation creeping in here)
17. Own a pair of handmade shoes
18. Try snowboarding
19. Travel to Australia (oh so future Emma is also rich now is she?)
20. Be a bridesmaid (so close)
21. Take a pottery class (come on, this one would have been easy)
22. Ride an elephant
23. Read every book I own cover to cover
24. Go on safari
25. Run a half marathon (ha)
26. Get a tattoo
27. Get a dog (I'm thinking one of the previous 26 should have been *Learn to look after self*)
28. Fly first class
29. Live abroad
30. See the Taj Mahal

It seemed such a great idea at the time. Now it's like 30 monkeys hanging off my back to remind me of how little I've achieved. When I was younger people in their thirties always seemed so grown up, so together, so accomplished, but now I know they were probably bricking it like I am.

And then it dawns on me my biggest achievement this year has been coping. Getting up every morning and carrying on. And because of my resilience I've come through it relatively unscathed and able to spend the rest of my life working through this list.

Screw it. I'm adding 20 more and making it a before I'm 50 list. Suck on that monkeys.

P Day + 89

Tonight's birthday celebrations were a sweat fest. And not just me for a change.

There's something going on with my internal thermostat that means I'm either a shivery, teeth chattering, goose pimpled wretch or a sweaty, wet patch sporting fruity smelling beast. They say that ladies don't sweat, they perspire. I call bollocks on this. I sweat. Perspire is too elegant a word for what's going on now down my back.

Whatever we're calling it it's been happening a lot recently. I'm never a sensible temperature, never just right. This summer hasn't helped so far by being ridiculously muggy. Every day is clammy. It keeps hurling it down with rain but it's like a bloody rainforest and never cools.

I've had train journeys where I seem to have my own climate, where other commuters look cool as cucumbers and I'm moist. I've been sat in the sun drinking hot chocolate under a blanket. I never know what amount of clothing to put on so carry layers to bulk up or strip down at various points of the day. It's a permanent battle that I'm definitely losing.

Tonight, for my thirtieth celebration, I have chosen a bar that seems to be down in the earth's core, where the lava is, it's that hot. With air con which seems to be so warm and sleepy itself that it can only lazily waft out semi-chilled air in a two centimetre radius below its vent. People are actually popping out every other drink to treat themselves to a beer in the temperature controlled bar across the road. The rest of us who've decided to see it through are fanning ourselves with menus, dabbing our foreheads with the hems of our summer dresses and drinking cocktail after cocktail after cocktail as if they might hydrate us. One friend just left a conversation mid sentence, threw up, and returned to the chat without missing a beat. Another just asked the DJ to play Backstreet Boys. That's how weird the heat's making us.

I treat myself to a few minutes under the lethargic air conditioning, I look around and I notice two things. The first is how nice it is to have all your favourite people in one room. It's so rare to be able to get everyone together. And secondly how across the board totally and utterly hammered everyone is. There's not one single person without a goofy, gin soaked expression on their face. We've definitely all mistaken the contents of these twee vintage tea cup cocktails as being as genteel as their containers. A lot of people are going to be very ill tomorrow.

And I realise one more thing. They're all here for me. They're stood in this hot as hell room because I asked them to. And I know in that instant I'm sweaty but I'm loved.

It's my party and I'll perspire if I want to.

Hangover food is crisps. Bacon. Cola. Leftover pizza/ kebab/burger. Whatever that is that's been festering in the back of the fridge for a week. Hangover food is not cake. Well not for me anyway. Cake is civilised, deserves a proper plate and a clean liver, and shouldn't be consumed on top of Jägerbombs.

My parents are taking me for afternoon tea for my birthday which is lovely, but after last night's cocktail fest I need something savoury. I stuff as many mini elegant sandwiches as I can into my mouth to soak up the gin that's now sloshing around with the cup of tea I've just sipped. By the fourth quarter sandwich I think I'm cake ready; the thought of icing isn't making me retch which is progress.

My nan seems oblivious to my bloodshot eyes and the faint whiff of sambuca on my breath. I've been reciting *Don't throw up in front of Nan, don't throw up in front of Nan, don't throw up in front of Nan* to the point that I'm struggling not to blurt it out, but I think I've just about pulled it off. But now she's handing me a huge plate of scones, jam and cream so I may have spoken too soon.

P Day + 92

So I go to see the nurse at my local docs about something completely Little P unrelated (ok if you must know, pill injection, if I am going to get addicted I should at least be protected) and I get into my regular rant about paying for prescriptions yadda yadda. She asks me who the Parkinson's prescription is for, I say me, her eyes widen in a *reeeeeaaaalllly* sort of way, my eyes roll in an *oh god here we go* kind of way, but she doesn't start a reel of questions, she's not over keen to know every detail, she just says *I would never have known* and I instantly love her.

She then starts telling me if I want to have kids I should probably get cracking then she jabs the needle with the contraceptive into my hip. Ah I love irony.

For as long as I can remember I've been scared of fairground rides. It's almost indiscriminate; roller coasters, carousels, waltzers, bumper cars, big wheels are all on my *flat out no* list. It's not the speed or the twisting and turning, although that doesn't help, it's the fear of slipping out. Ridiculous I know, there's usually safety bars that hem you in and stop that. I just had a couple of hairy experiences when I was younger that mentally scarred me for life and led to me being the wuss that I am.

When I was at college I had a boyfriend whose family routinely took a trip to Blackpool each summer. One year I went with them. We played the slots, ate fish and chips and by night had our melon vodka shots spiked by dodgy foreign men (but that's a story for another chapter). All good so far until it was suggested we explore the Pleasure Beach.

Not since *The NeverEnding Story* has a name been more misleading.

There were rides. Death machines. Lots of them. Varying shapes, sizes and themes but all masquerading as fun. Bright colours and jolly typefaces to hide the massive descents and huge swing radius. To lots of people I'm sure this would be exciting and at this point I was open minded, I'd try a few things to appease the family, all big death machine fans, and then scuttle away to find some chicken nuggets.

Ride 1: Innocent looking carousel

Just a regular carousel. Candy coloured horses with fake flowing manes and golden poles to hold onto. It looked like a good entry level ride for a scaredy cat. Slow, with some gentle up and downing, pretty music as a distraction and my horse was an ebony beauty called Rainbow, strap me in, how wild could this possibly get. Turns out Rainbow was a bit of a dark horse in more ways than one and I ended up as green as the ribbon on her deceptively carefree tail.

Ride 2: Fun looking horse race

With a half remembered phrase about getting back on the horse after falling off one milling round my head I went on a quest for a more noble steed. I found a child's steeplechase ride, ten horses racing around a track through artificial greenery. The children seemed to be loving it so I thought it was a safe bet. It wasn't. The children were liars. The whole way round I felt like I was sliding off it. And I finally got to the end and the bastard thing went round again. Twice.

Ride 3: My first ever roller coaster

Feeling like things couldn't get worse I thought I'd tackle the big one. And by the big one I mean the children's roller coaster. I got into the carriage, the safety bar lowered down towards my lap and stopped about three feet in front of me. I waited in case it would move closer but it didn't. This ride was clearly made for obese children and I wasn't one of those so I started to panic. There was no way this bar was going to hold me in enough but I gripped onto it with steely determination and got ready for the car to start its climb. What followed is probably hands down the closest I've ever come to soiling myself in public. I was petrified, the bar was useless and the ride had more twists and turns in it than your average *EastEnders* episode.

I've never been on another ride since.

Today the new boy and his friends want to go on the RIB (a small inflatable boat that goes very fast up the Thames) and I, against my better judgement, am going with them. At least if I slide out of it I'll just land in the Thames rather than head first onto concrete or underneath a plastic horse.

P Day + 102

The new fun challenge – keeping shoes on.

I'm like one of those kids who sits in a pushchair kicking their shoes off and their mum doesn't realise until they've got on the bus/left the shop/pulled out of the motorway lay-by. Drunk adults don't seem to be much better at it. You see lone shoes in the weirdest places. I like to make up little stories about how the trainer got in the tree, how the stiletto ended up on top of McDonald's and how the beautiful boots ended up in my shopping cart on ASOS.

The thing is, I'm supposedly an adult and as far as I'm aware I'm not drunk, but little p seems to think its hilarious to kick my shoes off at the most inopportune moments. Recent occurrences have been in a client meeting (*Oops let me just pick that up*), running for a bus (*Wait for meeeeee*), on said bus a few minutes later (*Wait for meeeee part deux*) and in my own lounge with a particularly troublesome pair of slippers (*too many expletives to pass editing*). Luckily, being an adult I can just put them back on so little p can, hilariously, continue the game.

I need some of those sexy Velcro trainers I had when I was 15 and I wore cycling shorts and global hyper Technicolor t-shirts.

There's a lot of debate about when people should start taking medication for Parkinson's. They're pretty nasty drugs and there's not many types of them so you don't want to use all your options too quickly. Some people stay off them as long as they can to prolong the effectiveness. I was given the choice and decided to start treatment.

Weirdly I've been excited about starting to take something, anything – *give me all the drugs*. I haven't felt like I'm fully in control of the condition so far, it's been a bit raw, and I'm ready to start chemically fighting it as hard as I'm mentally fighting it. I've earmarked today as a good day to take my first doses; it's a weekend, we have no plans and my snuggliest tracksuit bottoms are fresh from the dryer. Let's pop some pills and do some lounging.

The leaflet inside the pack reads like *War and Peace* so I skip to the good stuff, the side effects:

Very common:
abnormal movements
headache

Common:
abdominal pain
fall
fever
flu
general feeling of being unwell

chest pain
joint pain
numbness and muscle weakness of the hand
abnormal dreams
difficulty in muscular coordination
depression
dizziness
prolonged muscle contractions

Uncommon:
stroke
heart attack

Jesus christ! Most of these things are WORSE or the same as the symptoms I'm trying to control! And they say that strokes and heart attacks are uncommon but they're common enough to bother to print them on the leaflet. Why have I been so excited about this? I suddenly feel the same as when I was told Santa isn't real. The medication I've pinned all my hopes on might make me feel horrendous rather than fix me and that's so terrifying I consider not taking them for a microsecond.

9am: down the hatch. They're the only option I have.

11am: I feel the same, maybe a little bit tired but I was out late last night. If this is how it's going to be this is fine and they need to do some serious rewording of the pamphlet. I'm a little disappointed that I can't feel them working.

1pm: I retract that last statement. They're doing something, perhaps not the right thing: I don't think the right thing was to make me so nauseous it's as if I've downed six melted cartons of Ben and Jerry's. I don't think the right thing was to make my head feel like someone's been using it for boxing practice. I definitely don't think the right thing was for me to not be able to feel my legs.

2pm: is there a way to un-take tablets when they're in your system?

3pm: I can't feel anything from the waist down so the waist up is frightened. I'm lying in bed not moving a muscle, like I'm playing Dead Lions all by myself, and I can feel my heart trying to escape because it's scared like I am.

4pm: I can't believe I'm spending a beautiful sunny day laying flat out on my bed. I hate these tablets already and we have a whole life together in front of us, I can see it not being a happy relationship. One of us is already taking the piss. One of us is making the other feel like they have the flu, a migraine, a tummy bug, no legs and a scared heart all at once.

5pm: Screw this, I'm going to the pub. It won't matter that I can't feel my legs there. No one else can feel theirs, either.

P Day + 104

Someone once said that insanity is doing the same thing over and over and over and expecting something different to happen. I think that sounds like optimism, or maybe they're just the same thing.

So I guess it's optimistic insanity that makes me put the same tablets in my mouth today that yesterday made me feel god awful. That makes me take a massive glug of water and swallow them down. That makes me think today they might work and not just make me vomit.

When you're curled up under your desk at work because it 'looks comfy' you know you're in a bad way.

I would consider myself usually a fairly energetic, upbeat, positive kind of person. The glass of gin is always half full with me. But since I've started taking these meds I'm that, but cranked up to 11 which is exhausting. I permanently feel like I've drunk ten Red Bulls which is particularly troublesome when stuck in a meeting room or trying to sleep, things which sometimes go hand in hand.

I'm taking the tablets with breakfast so my stomach's lined which means I get a solid four hours between getting up and taking them where I am Jekyll, feeling brilliant, calm, productive, cheery. I take the tablets at 10:30 and within an hour I'm Hyde, a negative, cranky, yet hugely hyperactive ball of mess that wants to punch everything. It's the oddest sensation. I can feel the medication streaming through my brain and firing off to all the muscles. My body is tired but my muscles think it's party time and are demanding we do star jumps and jazz hands and high kicks. *Not now, muscles, we're working.* And in bed my brain is tired but my muscles think it's exercise time and are demanding we go running and jumping and punching. *Not now, muscles, we're sleeping.*

At work I'm likely to get myself a kidney infection from the amount of times I'm getting up and walking around on the pretext of needing a wee, diabetes from all the sugary tea I'm making, sacked from talking too much to my colleagues.

And now at 2pm I find myself on the floor. I've deflected the weird looks to my desk buddy who is probably going to be socially shunned for spending the afternoon chatting to the carpet.

With no hint of irony the words *What better day to wear a metallic skirt than the day you see your Parkinson's nurse?* left my mouth this morning. I could have passed it off as side effects but to be honest I've always fought life's uncertainties and dramas with sequins.

Today three brilliant things happened (other than the skirt).

I saw my nurse

Two people thought I was 20

I had the best chocolate caramel shortbread of my life

I'll address these in order of importance.

1.   The shortbread was incredible. My god, it looked good on its little tray and I thought it's worth a punt because sometimes caramel shortbread can be heartbreakingly disappointing – but this one didn't let me down. I sat outside the hospital after all my escapades with a hole in my arm, a stitch in my stomach, a system coursing with medication and a smile on my caramel streaked face.

2.   The first age mistake came from super nurse's colleague. I wish I could remember her name, it's at that awkward point where I've met her at least once and now can't ask her what it is. To be fair the first

time was on P-Day and that's no time for pleasantries. But anyway we were all chatting, I was aware I was buzzing a little bit off the meds and felt like the only drunk at a party and she just threw it in. *You look so young, I'd say you could pass for 20.*

Yes! Score! Result!

It happened again when I was just about to have my blood stolen by a zealous phlebotomist and she wrote my birth year as 1993; ok she didn't actually say it but she didn't correct it and that counts.

3. Super nurse is like the Challenge Anneka of the neurological world and I swear she's more important to me than cake really. Set her any task or problem and she'll solve it. A mere flash of a dubious rash that my local nurse was flummoxed by and I'm making an unscheduled visit down to the dermatology ward. This is why she's my hero and why I now find myself 90 minutes and one biopsy later wondering if you ate too many caramel shortcakes whether you'd split a stitch open.

When we were little we had the best holidays. And thanks to my dad and the technology boom of the eighties they're all on video, and now thanks to my nan, transferred onto DVD (I have no idea how she knows how to do this stuff). To avoid the inevitable shameful first airing at my future, non existent wedding I armed myself by watching them all through.

I was struck by two things.

1. I needed the toilet and didn't go a lot which resulted in a strange contorted dance and the other kids yelling *Emma needs a wee* at key moments.

2. I was a regular kid. There was no sign that anything was different (apart from an extraordinarily powerful bladder). And I guess at that point there wasn't. I'm rubbish at diving, that's a given, I'm a Lawton, but apart from that I look strong and fast and ridiculously skinny.

Time to get as strong as a ten year old again.

You know that feeling when you watch something on YouTube you shouldn't and you immediately want to wash out the inside of your brain with industrial strength bleach? Fess up, we've all done it. Someone sends you a link and you open it out of curiosity and regret it almost instantly, the grossness/sadness/nakedness of it imprinting itself on your retina to keep replaying itself as you go about your day. I'm sat in a PYSD (Post YouTube Stress Disorder) daze, disbelieving of what I've just seen, tears streaming down my face, both cursing and thanking my rabid curiosity for clicking on the link in the harmless looking email from a friend.

I'd heard it spoken about before but never seen it happen, never witnessed it almost first hand, never realised its power. Deep Brain Stimulation. DBS. Three little letters that in the Parkinson's world command almost as much faith and belief as another three letter word I don't believe in. I'm putting my faith in medicine.

Here's the science bit.

DBS is a surgical procedure used to treat symptoms like tremor, rigidity, stiffness, slowed movement, and walking problems. A thin, insulated wire is pushed through a small opening in the skull and implanted in the brain. The tip of the wire is positioned within a particular brain area depending on the patient and their symptoms. A sort of extension cable is passed under the skin of the head, neck, and shoulder, connecting the lead to the battery pack which is placed near the collarbone.

Here's the non science bit.

It's magic.

I've just watched a man on the other side of the world, angular and shaking like a leaf, flick a switch on his DBS control and become still, soft, human. I'm terrified and excited all at the same time. Because the before and after I've just witnessed are both my future.

P Day + 112

Solicitors aren't human beings, I'm pretty much sure of it. Mine just told me she exchanged contracts on my flat on Friday morning. *Friday!* It's Monday morning now, why did she not tell me on Friday so I didn't worry all weekend and when it would have been socially acceptable to get ratted to celebrate.

P Day + 117

I've always been a fast walker. I take after my dad who routinely almost got the entire family run over on our yearly Christmas outing to London.

Now I live in the city (ok fair point I don't at this precise moment, but I technically own a house there now so let me off yeah) I love pacing through its streets, pushing tourists to the side, no idea where I'm going, no chance of me consulting a map. I've got a bit slower lately and it bugs me to high hell, it's more of a shuffle with the odd poor attempt at a sprint if my bus is leaving or there's a long platform and I'm at the wrong end (the two situations where it is acceptable to run... Ok maybe if you hear rumour that a new TK Maxx is opening, three). So I was pretty chuffed to notice that I was back to my old pace today, sadly the medication has upped the speed I talk at too to pilled up raver so little victories will have to do for now.

I upped my medication dose yesterday, so today I'm stood on a train platform shoving crackers into my gob like my life depended on it just to stop myself being sick. Because I doubt if I was sick people would think *Oh bless her, she clearly has Early Onset Parkinson's and she's just upped her dose of Ropinirole, let me hold her hair... back.*

They'd judge me, they'd think I'd had a roaring Saturday night on the sauce, they'd think I'd been doing vodka shots off the chest of a half naked bar man, they'd think I'd fallen into bed fully clothed with a dirty kebab by my side. Jeez. I really need to get a better life.

P Day + 119

There is a moment in every girl's life where she gets over excited about the range of soft drinks available at a pub. I hoped I'd be at least 45 or pregnant before this kicked in but no I am now that girl.

Don't get me wrong, I've not gone completely TT. I checked with super nurse and she laughed at me, a proper deep guffaw, so that means *Don't be an idiot. Half the people I work with are buzzing off their t***s, what harm can a cider do?* Or that's what I took it to mean. The medication said *Drinking is not recommended with these tablets* which seems open to negotiation, plus I don't plan on taking them *with* gin. I'll leave it at least five minutes.

Apparently chicken curry increases dopamine. It's something to do with the double whammy of protein rich chicken and lots of spices. Might explain why I feel so chipper today as I stuffed myself with it last night. 7pm I was being sick from the meds. 7:05 I was face deep in chapattis and lamb keema.

When I was a kid my mum used to take me to the doctors and say *She's sick* and the doc would say *Ok, anything in particular* and she'd say *I don't know but she's not eating*. I only stop eating for near death type illnesses, my arm would have to be falling off so I quite literally cannot lift the fork before I'd give in. I've eaten through glandular fever, food poisoning, colds, flu, tonsillitis and now I'm eating through Parkinson's.

I am hardcore.

I'm feeling really rough from the meds and the thought of traipsing into town just to have a dermatologist say *You still have a rash* doesn't appeal but I have to get this damn stitch taken out. Five minutes on Google, some sterilised tweezers and a pair of nail scissors later – problem solved.

I've always had a worryingly cavalier DIY attitude towards health, I once cut a giant splinter out of my foot when I was 15 using a scalpel and gallons of TCP. I pulled a shard of glass out of my uni housemate's foot because all the boys were wussing out. And now I'm not just qualified in feet, I've broadened my skills to stomachs too.

Do you reckon you can get DIY deep brain stimulation kits on eBay? I've got a set of tweezers and nail scissors primed and ready for action.

I've always liked the way that cats sit. How they tuck all their limbs in and wind in their tails and become a compact unit. It's probably one of the only things I like about them. Snooty little buggers.

I'm finding I feel least wobbly when all my limbs are closest together, if it was socially acceptable to crouch down in the foetal position on a train I'd do it. Because commuting is my bugbear at the moment. My parents live around an hour's train journey from the city and I, like so many others, cram myself into a carriage, position myself under the raised armpit of a fellow traveller and go into a sort of daze to remove myself mentally from the situation. But it's becoming more difficult though as I get more shaky to find something to hold onto, there's limited bars to grab and there's usually some arsehole leaning against the ones that are at my height. So often I'm like some overdressed surfer, knees slightly bent, arms steadying myself, riding the wave of a track merge near Luton.

If there is something to hold onto the fear of someone seeing me reach my shaking, uncertain claw out to clamp onto it fills me with dread. Kids see it and tell their mum. Teenagers see it and stare. Grown-ups see it and pretend they haven't. I feel like I look really dodgy, or ridiculously nervous like I've never taken the train before. So I reach out quickly, cover it with my other hand to hide the shaking and pull myself in close to the bar so I'm catlike and steady.

A neat little unit.

And I feel safe and compact and like even a fast approach to the platform at St Albans couldn't rock me. Until some smart suited pillock makes me move down the carriage and the whole process starts again.

P Day + 124

Since super nurse said the medication could send me a bit crazy in the buying things department I've been saying the words *I ordered it before I started the tablets* so often I should probably get it put on a t-shirt... ooh I need new t-shirts. My mum laughs nervously every time an ASOS or Debenhams or eBay parcel arrives but a girl needs new things for a new house and can't show her new house up with old clothes. I think everyone needs reminding I was like this before. I'm just trying to stay true to myself, I won't let Parkinson's change me.

The hugest John Lewis van pulled up outside the house today. Mum didn't say a word but I could tell she'd seen it through the net curtain by the sharp intake of breath that came from the next room. It took two burly men lifting beds and wardrobes by the dozen into the new house opposite to calm her.

I am actually in the market for a nice wardrobe. Best get that t-shirt made up.

P Day + 125

It was one of my friends' thirtieth birthday shindigs last night and there was obligatory fancy dress. I love when it's the law. I take after my parents in that I can't do half arsed when it comes to costumes. If an invite states fancy dress you'll find me up until all hours stitching sequins onto a mini skirt or eBaying for the tackiest fuschia wig.

When we were kids our school subjected us to what now seems like an excessive amount of days needing costumes. My parents, both artists, went crazy over this and constructed full battleships out of card for my brother and mermaid tails and shell bras for me. Looking back these costumes were awesome, lovingly constructed, each shiny scale on the tail stitched on by hand, each chimney on the battle ship bent into shape around a rolling pin. In any photos of these costumes we're both either sulking or crying (the parents must have been freaking out that the tears would make the colour on the cardboard run).

I took this high level of arty fartyness with me to uni and started to collect together a box which became known by my housemates as Emma's Crafty Bits. The night before any costume parties the box would be raided and we'd all be sat on the floor making scout badges out of felt or moustaches out of pipe cleaners. Our true moment of glory was when we constructed ammunition belts out of bits of fabric and tampons painted silver.

After uni my craft box dried up, I stopped making so many costumes and turned to the bought kind. I invested in a horrible matted long black wig from a costume store bargain bin and a pair of sequin leggings. I pretty much for a year tried to shoehorn these two items into any theme that was proposed.

Music stars: Amy Winehouse. Done.

Narnia: Evil witch. Done.

Roller disco: Eighties person with big hair and sequin leggings. Done.

I didn't even really like the costume very much but it dropped bits of matted hair and sequins on my friend's floor and the subsequent moaning was well worth it.

One night returning from Karaoke dressed as Miss Winehouse and Elton John we stumbled across a girl who was about ten Malibus past ok in the doorway of a shop. We checked she was alive, saw she was sparko, called an ambulance and put her into the *Don't die from being sick* position. She came round to see a pretty damn convincing Winehouse and Elton leaning over her. I'm sure that girl's had less weird nights.

This morning I've got bits of blue hair wrapped around my ears, glitter in my eye and blisters from dancing after spending the evening dressed as Katy Perry. I went all out. Fake eyelashes. Kitsch jewellery. Diabetes inducing make-up colours. Tacky high heeled shoes. Totally worth it as I won the costume competition. Mum and Dad would be proud.

P Day + 126

I'm getting very good at this.

What did you get up to this weekend.

*Ohnotmuchitsbeenabusyweeksoijustrestedandateand-
watchedalotofBreakingBadandihadtoupmydoseofmedica-
tiondidyouknowihaveParkinsonsihavetogoandgetmytrain-
nowillseeyoutomorrow.*

And I'm off, not even looking back to see the puzzlement.

I am a ninja P bomber extraordinaire. I can just slide it into chat like a pro now. I'm taking down work colleagues. *POW.* People at parties I haven't seen since school. *SMASH.* Random people in shops. *KABOOM.* Facebook friends. *KO.* It's becoming an obsession to see how subtly I can drop it in, a little game I play against myself.

Oh god... this isn't my addiction is it? Trust me to get a crap one. I was at least hoping to get good at blackjack.

P Day + 127

Can't believe I just bought a pill box. I'm not talking those vintage enamelled jobbies, I mean the horrible old person plastic ones that look like a poor man's Millennium Falcon. I've been struggling through, whipping out my tablets at work, trying to pop them out of their packages without them going on the floor, picking them off the floor, dusting them off (five second rule plus these things are about a quid a pop) and downing them slyly with an overhot cup of tea. I need to classy up this procedure somewhat if these slippery little buggers and me are going to have to be friends for life.

In my defence I chose pink plastic. Rock on.

I've been to Glastonbury enough times to know what someone on LSD looks like. All the old hippies, sometimes stark bollock naked, dance around, eyes glazed, loving the world and all its beauty.

That was me in a meeting today. Not naked, or dancing, god I'm not that bad yet. But I'd just taken my medication on a slightly empty tummy and rushed into this meeting, felt fairly sensible for the first ten minutes and then suddenly everything became brighter and clearer and sharper. The paper in front of me was hurting my eyes it was so bright, I wanted to play with my colleague's hair because it looked like cotton wool, my pen was burning deep dark lines into my notepad with every note I scribbled. It was cool. I sort of think I covered it by babbling something about websites and no one looked horrified, but my cheeks were burning and I felt giggly and like the meeting room was the most amazing thing I'd ever seen. For the record it's a pretty standard issue meeting room.

I told my colleague and he said he was excited because he had a meeting with me in five minutes. I was excited because it meant there might be a chance to stroke his beard.

I've always prided myself on being a minimal puker. I save it for special occasions only. That time I was in a cheesy nightclub and hurled up over the balcony onto the dance floor. The time I was eight and at school where I started a domino effect of vomity children in the reading corner. Or the time I peppered the stairs in my friend's new house with blackcurrant tinted stomach juice. Some of my finest moments. Two from alcohol, I'll let you guess which ones.

So it's been a teensie bit annoying that I've broken my winning streak this past week. I've been vomming like a trooper. Slight smell of toilet cleaner. YACK. One chip too many. YACK. Massive spot on a commuter's shoulder. DOUBLE YACK.

I've tried everything. Salty snacks. Dry crackers. Flat lemonade. The anti-sickness tablets they prescribed me. Acupressure travel sickness bands. Calming tincture. Aromatherapy wrist rollons. I even tried wine because, well, there's nothing that doesn't cure. No luck. I've been spending more time in the toilet at work than my colleague who used to nap in there. She clearly had a stronger stomach than me.

P Day + 131

Upping your dose of vomit inducing tablets on the same day you have a fitting of your very beautiful, probably pretty expensive bridesmaid dress feels like you're dicing with dry cleaning. Managed to hold back so I celebrated with a shortbread.

The dress is drapey and way more feminine and sophisticated than anything I own. And it's long, the sort of long you need heels for so you don't keep tripping up on it. I keep having nightmares that I wobble and fall just as we're walking down the aisle and as I freak out I grab both the other bridesmaids and the bride, her dad and the vicar and pull the whole bastard lot down with me.

So I'm on the lookout for a pair of wedges, the hero of shoes, high enough to feel special, sturdy enough not to floor an entire wedding party.

For someone who looks as scruffy as me I spend a disproportionate amount of time on grooming. I dye my hair a sort of purply red and I hate it when my boring plain-Jane brown roots show. I wear thick black eyeliner every day, I won't leave the house without it because people always ask if I'm ill if I do. I'm a nail art geek and think that a naked nail is a travesty. I spend hours at the weekend putting on face masks, curing gel on my toenails with UV light and seeking out stray eyebrows. Yet I still manage to look a mess. My hair is wiry and untamed, my face is pale in the bad non Pre-Raphaelite way, my nails chip within five minutes of painting them. I envy women that just look effortlessly groomed, immaculately preened, like they just woke up that way. If I was Parisian they'd have had me expatriated by now for letting the place down.

Every morning getting ready takes that little bit longer as I wobble my eyeliner into some sort of acceptable shape and then take it off and start again because I look as if I'm the fifth member of Kiss. I've always used liquid eyeliner because it's dark dark black and that's fun but by god it's unforgiving when your hand and eye are moving at two different speeds like two 12 year olds slow dancing at a school disco.

So why do I bother? I guess I just always have and there's no way I'm going to let little p turn me into a straggly haired, make-up abstaining, monobrow sporting, long skirt wearing (unless it's a midi length from Topshop) monstrosity. I had my teenage years for that.

P Day + 133

The tablets aren't working for me. It's pretty obvious. Super nurse says they should have stopped making me this nauseous by now and they should be making my Parkies easier to manage and they're not. The theory is that they're getting lost in my digestive system.

My stomach. Like the naughty kid at school you know it'll always be the one behind any sort of trouble. Ever since I was little it's let me down. When I was small I got salmonella poisoning from a chain restaurant and Mum says I struggled to shift it. I had to stay off school until it had gone and a man came round weekly to test my poo to verify when that was. Apparently it never fully left my system but Mum and The Poo Man decided it was safe for me to be around other kids while the last bit cleared up. According to countless tests in my adult life it never really did.

So super nurse and the Prof say I'm now a bigger challenge to them. Most of the medication is tablet form and right now we're going to have to write those off. Maybe I can try them again in the future but for now they're off the table. They start talking about a patch – *what like a smokers patch?* Apparently yes. I'd just pop it on my skin in the morning and for 24 hours it would deliver medication through my skin. No more remembering to take tablets throughout the day. No more stomach cramps. This sounds perfect.

Super nurse writes a note for my doctor and I feel hopeful.
Come on patch, you're my new best friend.

The patches are awesome. Apart from their dubious attempt at matching skin tone their makers did a sterling job. Sure, there's the usual terrifying list of side effects and a ridiculously complex diagram of where you can stick them but they're reducing a lot of the nasty things I was experiencing with the tablets. Apart from the nausea, that's a keeper.

Ten things I've learnt about the patches.

They're metallic on the back so get really hot if you stand too near the oven.
They leave a gross residue around their edges that won't budge even after a shower so you look permanently grubby.
They are visible if you wear a short skirt.
The tiny writing on them makes total strangers really intrigued and starey.
They hurt a lot if you put them on your stomach.
They're not sexy.
They sting if you have a bath.
The see through plastic backings they're stuck to hide on the carpet and block up the hoover.
If you forget to put a new one on after a few hours you feel really rank.
All of the above don't come close to mattering when they make your movement less jerky, your thoughts clearer and your speech less slurry.

Getting myself into a rhythm with them is proving difficult but I'll get there. It's nothing a few well placed Post-it notes and an alarm clock won't fix.

There are people in life who go for what is safe. And there are those who don't. And I've always found myself drawn to people who are unexpected, who break the mould a bit, who are always themselves no matter where they are and who they're with. I hope I'm at least a little bit like that too.

My friend from uni is a wonderful example. A petite Lebanese beauty, all softly curling dark hair and Bambi eyes. But if you for a second on meeting her assumed this would make her a pushover then you'd probably find yourself hobbling away with your balls in your hand. She's feisty, she's sharp as a tack and she loves a debate, and be under no illusions, she'd always win because she's smart.

There's the successful tech entrepreneur who everyone said was too big for his boots. There's the man who says very little but whose smile speaks volumes. There's my dad who lost a lot of his sight but has written a book, started a band and still plays golf. People like them make life more interesting.

The Managing Director at work, Hardip, is one of my favourite surprises. He's king of the spreadsheet, organised beyond belief and like soothing calamine lotion when it comes to talking to disgruntled clients. His flip side? He is totally and utterly obsessed with things that sparkle. Serious magpie.

Five fabulous facts about Hardip.

He puts on parties at work called Hardip Glitter Parties.
He renamed them Hardip's Sparkle Parties after he realised
there may be unwanted links between our shindigs and a
certain musical paedophile.
He owns disco lights, proper ones.
He wears fairy lights into work to cheer us up.
It took an hour for me to take his supposedly candid staff
photo because he wanted to get his diamanté phone case in
the shot and I didn't.

He's a one-off. Unique. He's a business man by day and a
talented artist by night/weekend but in both worlds he's
the same person and he fits because he doesn't try to if
that makes sense. He's just him. Tonight he's putting on a
party in our office because we need a treat. He'll string up
the lights, attach the glitter ball to the boardroom ceiling
and shake out the gold tablecloth. The shared Spotify
playlist is fully loaded. We've been discussing outfits all
week, him trying to outdo my sequin dress, and I've been
looking forward to blowing off some steam, I need gin and
Rihanna, stat.

But I can't. Because the nausea is unending and my head
feels like it's caving in and I can't face it. And again I'm
sat crying because I'm angry and frustrated and tired. It's
winning.

P Day + 145

I've been feeling extra shaky so super nurse said I could increase my dose of patches. She's really trusting and lets me manage my own medication. Most days I'm an adult and do it properly. One day in 20 I feel like sticking them all over myself to see what would happen.

P Day + 148

Jeez. I'm accumulating a lot of stuff. My new flat better be as it is in my head rather than how big it looks like on these accurate floor plans.

P Day + 149

Howard Marks step aside. There's a new drug lord on the scene.

I've just, without thinking, collected my prescription from Boots, and gone straight into a Pixies gig. Cool as a cucumber I've just strode casually past five burly security men with 100 doses of mind altering drugs in my satchel. They didn't even search me. I'm guessing Howard Marks never carried a satchel.

I'm in. I'm bloody in. I'm locking the door just in case they realise they've made a mistake and that they've left someone who doesn't know how to clean a bath properly, or work central heating or look after themselves in charge of a whole flat. Not just as a visitor but as its owner. I've never owned anything this good. Or been in charge of anything this expensive. *Eeeeeeeeek*.

I've been anxious since 8am when I left my parents' house to come into London and wait, for an agonising period of time, for the solicitor to confirm my mortgage money has been transferred across to the housing organisation and that they can let me through the door and give me the keys. Thankfully, for me, a friend is off work sick and sits with me in a local pub where I sip a lemonade and sneakily charge my phone.

And then I get the call and I'm so excited I pretty much float the whole five minute walk to the development, probably with a demented smile on my face. And they let me in. And tell me all about how to keep a bath clean, work central heating and look after myself but I'm not listening, I'm staring at the woman and in my head I'm screaming *ohmygodohmygodohmygodohmygod*. She hands me a big folder which I hope contains all the bath/heating/self user guides and she leaves.

And I wait for five minutes by the door in case she comes back, realising her mistake. But she doesn't.

In every new relationship there's a lot of first times. The first time you kiss. The first time you meet their friends. And the biggie. The first weekend away together.

The boy and I have worked together for years so we've had a fair few weekends away for Christmas parties and the like but never one where we were a couple and that just involved us and not 65 other drunk people. I'm nervous about it because it feels quite make or break, our first romantic trip will be the marker for all future excursions. We've found a beautiful apartment on the internet and even though I've literally just moved into my flat we're going to go and live in someone else's for a few days. We're planning nice dinners, lazing in coffee shops, over consumption of cheese and a float in a spa pool, what can go wrong?

I have a friend who tells me her first trip away with her now husband was also the first time she had food poisoning, the first time she locked herself in the bathroom for two hours, and the first time he heard her explode from both ends through the paper thin wall. Ah romance.

I hadn't thought about that. There's something weirdly groundbreaking about that first shared space, the first bed that you both curl up in for the first time and the first toilet you both curl one out in. I don't think I'm the first girl to have pretty much dodged any number 2s in his company for our first few months together, which with my stomach is a miracle. I don't think I can go a whole weekend though, I'd explode.

This weekend we've broken a whole range of firsts.

The first time he's seen me in a bikini.
The first time he realised I don't run for public transport.
The first time he witnessed my extreme levels of overpacking.
The first time he saw me change my medication patch.
The first time I heard him mention me on the phone to his parents.
The first time I knew for sure that he was a keeper.

P Day + 161

I just dyed my hair in my new flat. I must have nerves of steel.

P Day + 165

I never thought I'd see a male strip show.

I never thought I'd see a male strip show with my mum.

I never thought I'd see a male strip show with my mum and the thing that stopped me having to see the gyrating man's full undercarriage would be her sitting in the row in front of me and witnessing it all herself.

We're on my friend Lucy's hen weekend in Brighton. She's invited our mums and her aunties and it's really lovely having them here. We're spending time together during the day then going our separate ways later, us to a club, them home. It's working perfectly. Right up until the strip show.

I find things like that so awkward anyway. The girl sat next to me and I have come to the conclusion that it's not hot. I think I'd like a show where men put on a nice soft jumper and a pea coat. But instead there's a greased up guy draped with a Union Jack flag (I don't think the Queen would approve) feeding a banana to a blindfolded hen. It's so cringe. But a must for any bridal party if the pamphlet is to be believed.

I'm so glad my mum's here. Not only has the back of her head just protected me from full frontal but it's nice to have fun with her, it's been a tough year and we deserve it.

I'm having a why me sort of day. The kind of day when a cloud hangs above your head and even inanimate objects are out to get you. This seems to have been my base level for days now, my mood shifting slightly higher or lower than the line every so often but always returning.

I've been crying a lot. It's mostly frustration. At the Parkinson's for being an arsehole to me. At myself for letting it. At myself for crying. At myself for getting angry with myself for crying. Because crying doesn't solve anything, I'm still left with the same feelings after, I just have puffy eyes and blocked sinuses to boot.

I'm not depressed, or at least I don't think I am. I'm just weighing up everything I've been dealt. Contemplating my next move. Working out how to beat it. I'm not depressed. I'm fine. Or at least that's what I keep telling myself.

P Day + 174

Today I'm shaking the blues off in the style of a 1950s housewife. I have made a cushion cover, a cute little fabric picture and a chicken dinner. Winner winner.

P Day + 180

Another day another cancellation. *I can't come* is starting to trip out of my mouth more frequently than I'd like. I'm supposed to be going out of town for a friend's birthday dinner but I'm exhausted and emotional. I'm worried people are going to stop inviting me to stuff. Would you bother inviting the girl who always says no?

P Day + 181

It's very nice that they're building a pretty bridge I can see from my window and a wildlife garden for all the little homeless animals but seriously if whoever keeps digging and beeping outside my window keeps doing so at 7am I'm going to come down there and dig them a new hole.

P Day + 184

I meet Mum for a cuppa and I spill out my fears about becoming a loner who never goes anywhere. As it tumbles out of my mouth I realise how stupid it sounds. It's not even a real problem. It ranks alongside there being a shortage of quinoa in Waitrose. Other people would die to be in the situation I'm in, being invited to fun stuff by fun people. Oh no. The hardship. I just need to man up and start attending. You don't get to run my life little p.

You can't get much for a penny nowadays. Those brightly coloured sweets in jars are now 5p. A wee in a station costs 30p. The 1p coins clog up your wallet, hide down the side of the sofa and generally make a nuisance of themselves until you drag them down to Boots and feed every last one off them into the self service machine while a queue forms behind you.

Their most recent crime? Losing me my mortgage. I kid you not. I finally got through to the man who ruined my life (temporarily) by declining my mortgage and the reason he gave astounded me. When I was younger I had a small loan with them. I worked hard to pay it off and celebrated a victory when I made the last instalment. Somehow I overpaid. By a penny. But they closed the account and left me in credit. When they ran my credit check this came up and counted as a negative attribute, being an over payer, and I was declined. If I hadn't managed to secure a new mortgage I don't think I'd be finding this as hilarious as I am from the safe comfort of fiscal security.

I've framed that penny. To remind me to not ignore the small stuff, it's always the thing that you least expect to that bites you in the arse.

P Day + 187

When we were kids our school would put on the best fireworks night displays. We'd spend all week making a guy out of straw from a local farm and dressing him up. It wasn't unusual to hear dads exclaiming from the side of the bonfire *Didn't I used to have a shirt that colour?* or *Isn't that my best tie?* The mums would sell toffee apples and hotdogs from the grill and we'd all stand around, skin stinging from the heat of the fire and ooooh and aaaaaaah at the beautiful colours the fireworks made.

I still love fireworks now. The glittery ones especially, and the ones that sort of fizz in the sky. In my opinion there should be more fireworks occasions, like birthdays and Christmas and Fridays.

Tonight, armed with a little can of gin and tonic, I'm going to a display near my house. I think the gin classes up the proceedings a little and hopefully if I get really tipsy I'll see double the fireworks.

I don't ask for much in life. Something yummy to eat, people to share it with, a comfortable place to sit and a bed to rest my bones in at the end of the day. The last one has proved to be the most difficult to achieve. After ordering it months ago the frame I picked out has been out of stock and I've been patiently waiting, sleeping on a mattress on the floor, camping out in my own flat. This was fun for about a week.

Mum's been calling them every day since I moved in, she's on first name terms with the store manager they speak so often. And it did the trick because it's finally here. I have something to sleep on that's higher than 2ft from the floor.

We're getting there. This is starting to feel like home.

P Day + 191

It's been raining a lot and the river seems to be getting a bit high. I'm in two minds. Do I hide up here on the fifth floor, or run downstairs and see if Waitrose have noticed it too and started panic reducing all their cake.

I can understand how people become alcoholics.

When you have pain, proper pain, and you go for a drink with friends, it softens, and you feel like it's bearable. And you can laugh and joke and you feel more like yourself. It's easy to see how you could start to rely on it to numb the discomfort, how you could begin going out more, sometimes on your own, just for a quick one, how you could sometimes have a few glasses of wine when you get home, maybe finish the bottle. You can see how that could spiral into drinking before work, during work, in the evening, because it calms the shakes and stops the stiffness, temporarily, until you have to drink again.

I'm keeping my drinking in check because I can see how it starts and how it ends.

em...hic

x

P Day + 206

Some people know it's nearing the festive period when they see the Coca-Cola advert with the big red lorry. I know it's that time when the first person mails me about what I'm wearing to the Christmas party.

One of the hardest things about having a health condition is carrying on as normal. Getting up, getting ready, travelling, working, socialising, all become more difficult. Most of the time I can do what I need to do just maybe a little slower, but every so often I drop the ball and something has to give.

Today I feel so nauseous and I'm sat in a meeting that feels like it will never end. I can feel my eyes getting heavy, and the sickness rolling through me from forcing them to stay open is overwhelming. But I have to be chirpy and listen and suggest fun ideas when all I want to do is hang out in the toilet and retch.

The meeting ends and I slump at my desk for a bit, my face in a pile of paper. My heart feels like it's ready to explode. The back of my head feels like it's filled with concrete. My chest like I've pulled all the muscles in it. I don't know what to do. I call a Parkinson's nurse and she suggests it's anxiety but that I should get it checked at A&E, so I hail a taxi and head there. The driver keeps talking to me and all the time my heart's beating out of my chest and in my head I'm begging him to shut up but I answer politely. The traffic moves slowly but eventually we get there.

And after three hours of triage, consultants and ECGs, all the while my heart punching away at my rib cage, I'm apparently fine. My heart's a little fast but I'm fine. But that doesn't even come close to reassuring me because I don't feel fine, that was scary and my chest feels bruised as a memento. It's the proof of how scary it was. That and the ECG sticker that's stuck to my bra.

I keep wanting to P bomb strangers.

I sit on the train waiting for someone to ask me to vacate the seat reserved for people with disabilities. I dare them to ask if I'm ok. I'm fighting battles that don't even exist.

I think it's because I get on with having Parkinson's, I don't moan about it or expect special treatment. And sometimes I just want to shout and scream about it but I don't because I hate negativity. It eats you up.

Having a long term condition and how you deal with it reflects on you as a person. If you're dealing with it well you're *inspirational*. If you're not no one knows what the hell to do with you. Recently I've not been playing the game. I've been letting it win. I feel like the me who smiles and dances and jokes and wears bright colours and goes to things she's invited to slipping away quietly and I've barely even kicked up a fuss. Even I'm disappointed in myself.

Sat in my new flat, surrounded by beautiful things, with my family visiting for the first time I realise something. I've worked hard for my life. Everything in it is because of a choice I've made or a TK Maxx homeware sale I've been to. I've built this. If a person came into my home, broke everything I care about, hurt my family, held me hostage so I couldn't leave, threatened to destroy the life I've created for myself and the people I love, would I just let them and crumple in a corner resigned to the fact that things would be bad from now on? Would I slowly become Gail from *Coronation Street*? Like hell I would.

So why is it that I've let an illness do that? Is it because it didn't have a face when it burst through the door? Hands to break things? A mouth to yell at my family? Arms to hold me down? I didn't know how to deal with a thing that couldn't be fought to the ground so I've done nothing. I've let a nothing take me down without a fight.

Ding ding round two.

P Day + 211

Cold medicines. Pretty harmless you'd think. Little boxes of hugs when you feel like a zombie came in the night and sewed your head onto its body. To me they're evil. Mainly because I'm yet to find one that doesn't make me feel worse. Hot drinkable medicine makes me cry. Tablets make me run around. Syrup makes me sick. All not welcome additions to my already irritating symptoms.

So I drink my weight in orange juice, breathe a steam of decongestant and make toddies of lemon, honey, ginger and rum. And the cold stays where it is. There's no getting rid of it. It must really like rum.

P Day + 212

It amazes me how little self awareness some people have. I think I've always swung a little too much the other way. Not all the time mind. I wear coats with polka dots on for christ's sake I can't be that judgemental of myself. But in life I'm one of life's fretters.

Case in point, that woman that's staring at me on the escalator, why does she hate me so much, does she know I've just got on the train without touching in my Oyster, I know I did it I was just rushing to make the train and my friends waiting for me at the other end and DON'T JUDGE ME OK IT'S BEEN A REALLY STRESSFUL DAY. What a bitch.

I'm permanently aware of my existence, of my personal space, if my bag is slightly too big, if I look dodgy, if one sock is slightly higher than the other, if I forgot to say thank you, if people think I'm a bad person, a bad friend, a bad daughter, a bad designer, a bad neighbour, a bad dresser, a bad decorator of my own home, a bad fellow commuter... The list is endless of all the people I'm trying not to offend.

And I'm equally judgemental of others and that's horrid. Not of my friends mind you, or my family, or my work colleagues, they could pretty much run up, slap me in the face, kick me in the shin and run away laughing and I still wouldn't judge them for it. But a stranger, they only have to hold me up on the escalator and they're my new nemesis, take the last reduced sausages in Waitrose and they get my death stare, talk loudly on their mobiles on the train and I'm planning a slow and painful vendetta involving cocktail sticks. And I was never like that, I used to be a nice girl, and I partially blame London and its selfish need to be the first on the train, the quickest through the barrier and off to your destination.

But in another positive swoop I wasn't expecting from Parkinson's I have suddenly become blaringly aware that every Londoner is a person, bumbling their way through a life which can be horrible and brilliant all at once, and their priority might not be to walk quickly through the turnstile or see who else is ogling the pack of sausages before they put them in their trolley.

I'd hate for anyone to judge me for walking too slowly up steps or packing my bags at a glacial pace in the supermarket. I do that enough myself.

P Day + 213

The cold I finally managed to get rid of yesterday to much whooping and celebration has made a surprise return. Touché cold. You are a worthy adversary.

P Day + 214

Tomorrow's the big day. One of my closest friends is going to be a wife and I have the honour of making her last walk as a single woman alongside her. I'm ready to burst with excitement. But there's a worry deep down in my tummy that I'll let her down. It's turned perceptibly colder overnight and I don't want to spoil her big entrance by everyone looking at the human jelly she's walked in with. And what if I drop the hymn sheet? Or the photos have motion blur around me?

Shut up little p it's not all about you.

P Day + 215

I have no voice. And not in a sexy way. In a I've smoked 70 a day for my whole life, Dot Cotton sort of way. On the one day I need to be elegant and demure I'm hacking up phlegm like a coal miner.

Thankfully Lucy's organised for us to have our hair and make-up done and after a vat full of foundation, a kilo of blusher and a mimosa I look and feel more human. We all slip into our dresses, beautiful long navy flowing numbers, and help Lucy into hers. She's stunning, like she was born to be a bride, and we wipe our happy tears away from our heavily blackened lashes.

And as we climb out of the classic car and walk her up to the church and down its aisle I feel like I'm smiling so wide my face might crack. I don't think I've ever been prouder. Of her. Of myself. Of our friendship that's weathered a fair few storms. It's a huge honour to be there for her on such a big day.

It's the perfect wedding, a gorgeous service, no one falls over and as we gather to have our photos taken I'm shaking like a leaf in the winter air but it doesn't matter. I'm warm on the inside, I've done her proud and photos don't show the shakes.

P Day + 216

I may feel sick as a dog today but thanks to industrial strength wedding hairspray I look like a glam pinup from the forehead up.

P Day + 221

Burping loudly into a sick bag in front of your work colleagues. It's right up there on the cringeometer.

We're all on a plane going to our Christmas party in Amsterdam (our company does celebrations in style) and I'm so sick. I think it's a combination of getting up early and fear of flying, whatever it is, the rowdy plane full of my excited workmates is making my head spin and as we take off I feel that watery feeling in the front of my mouth and a cold sweat starts to break and I grab for the sick bag and I open my mouth and I burp into it. A growly beast of a belch. And everyone hears it.

I won't be living this one down anytime soon.

P Day + 223

When you're in a place like Amsterdam it's apparently very easy to lose your mind. You can get pretty much anything you want, whenever you want it, and the place buzzes with the excitement of knowing that.

What with being on some hefty medication I'm barely touching alcohol at the moment and with Amsterdam not renowned for clean living I'm at a loose end. So I go shopping, my fail safe, and I find some Dutch pottery for my flat.

I'm so cool. Everyone else in Amsterdam is buying pot. I'm buying pots.

P Day + 227

When I moved into my new flat there were loads of other people moving into the building at the same time. You very quickly start to recognise faces, in the lift, by the mailboxes, on the nearby station platform and you feel sort of awkward that you never say hello, because you don't really know them.

So I'm grateful to the person who set up a Facebook group, who put a little note in everyone's mailbox and who got us all together in the pub tonight. You can never have too many friends.

I'm worried people might think I'm a WAG.

Most of the time I muddle through, try to do things myself, carry the shopping bags, reach the high cupboard. But as much as I hate it there are times I have to ask for help. And it's always the time there's someone nearby to overhear and judge me quietly for being a spoilt princess. There'll be 29 times I struggle to do up my coat but the one time I give up and let my work colleague do it because I'm all fumbly and we're late for a meeting you can bet your life the new guy will look up from his computer.

We've just bought our Christmas tree and as we walked off the man gave me the look. Because the boy is carrying the tree home and all of our shopping while a small handbag dangles off my wrist. I'm a modern woman and this is not ok. So in a display of defiance, and to the bafflement of the boy, I start to grab at the tree, tufts of needles coming off in my hand. So I make a lunge for the trunk and for a minute I'm supporting it a little bit, I think, and then I realise it's futile, I'm only hindering, and I look back to check the man's not looking and let go. And with a flick of my handbag I'm off down the road with my human pack horse in tow.

Today is my dad's birthday so I'm heading home on the train. I love going home to see my family and one thing in particular makes it extra special. Shaking my dad's hand.

Before you worry, no we're not some formal greeting, *good day Father* saying, curtsying, not a hair out of place, creepy as hell, kids grow up to be axe murderers type of family. It's just a routine that's grown out of me being a shaky. Before I was diagnosed my dad used to shake my hand to gauge how weak it was and tut under his breath that I still hadn't seen a doctor. And since the diagnosis I swear he's been using it as a sneaky yardstick to see whether I'm stronger. I can bounce into a room, beaming smile covering the fact I've barely slept, chirpy voice masking the voice tremor, teetering heels to disguise the wobbles but one handshake and he'll see right through me.

I've never been a physically strong person, I could kid myself and say that it's all gone downhill since the Parkies but at school I was always A for effort but E for achievement in gym. I've never been able to do the monkey bars. I refuse point blank to run for buses.

But that A for effort has held me in good stead this past year. My mental strength is growing to hulk proportions and I seem to be able to will my muscles to behave in an epic battle of mind over matter. If I go to say something and I stumble I stop, take a breath and try again. If my leg freezes I pause, imagine stepping over an imaginary object to CTL ALT DELETE my brain and we're back on the road again. If I can't open something I will my boyfriend out of his chair and into the kitchen. It's pure magic.

Speaking to a friend who is a personal trainer it's surprising to hear this is something he uses with his clients. Before they attempt a pull up he describes the muscles they'll use to do it and then their brains chomping at the bit to get going and gets all the relevant bits ready. It reminds me this is a brain thing, not a muscle thing ultimately, and brain things you can't necessarily cure but by hell you can try and outwit them.

So I'll see my dad today and I'll go into that handshake with all the planning and mental stamina of a boxer and the pay-off will make my year. The smile on his face that says he knows I'm doing ok.

P Day + 234

I've been following a no alcohol during the week rule, just until Christmas mind you, I'm not crazy. I feel like I'm boring everyone including myself. Not drinking makes you look like you don't know how to have fun, or are pregnant, and I'm not sure which of those horrifies me most.

P Day + 235

It's midnight and I'm shopping. This in my opinion, is the evil of modern technology, a blessing and a curse, that everything is so easily accessible whenever the mood strikes. Late at night I'm tired and low on dopamine and to get some quickly I need a rush of some kind. And online shopping provides that. I fill my basket with endless garments I pretend I'm buying and that gives me a fix, the thought of owning all these beautiful things, dresses I have no occasion for, shoes that would cripple me. It's harmless as far as I can see. I'm not spending any money and it makes me feel better so I can sleep. But tonight I've pressed Pay Now and logged into my PayPal and bought the items in my basket. And as soon as the order goes through I cancel it. It's like roulette. But this time there's too much of a buzz and I'm lying awake worried about what's just happened and whether it'll happen again. It can't happen again. I'm not letting it.

My acting past means I've always been able to cry on cue. But I've been doing so much of the real thing recently that I haven't needed to.

Don't feel sorry for me. It's not Parkinson's that's making me cry, it's bloody adverts. Loads of them. All sorts. Some designed to make you emotional, others so factual that I'm not even really watching them. But my tear ducts are. They're always watching, waiting for an African child or small kitten or wedding dress to flash up on the screen.

TV shows and films don't miss out on the waterworks. All I can say is it's lucky for my street cred that they're making films in 3D nowadays and I can hide behind the glasses.

P Day + 237

My wardrobes have finally arrived and I'm helping (supervising) the boy while he puts them together. At one point he's actually inside one of them (to many jokes about coming out of the closet) he's that thorough. I do the glory bits like hinges and hanging bars and you better believe I'm taking credit for all his work when my parents arrive in a few days.

I'm officially the flat pack queen. I should be the face of IKEA.

P Day + 238

My new wardrobes helped me select an appropriately sparkly outfit for my last day at work before Christmas. Now things are hanging up rather than strewn in plastic tubs it's a little easier.

On close inspection, when outside in daylight, I think the sequin top I've chosen might have seen better days, back when I was a bit more of a social butterfly it was a staple, and there's the faintest whiff of gin to it and what looks like ketchup on the hem. It's also really noisy, it's covered in those big round flat sequins that sort of make a *shhhhh shhhhh* noise when you walk. You *shhhhh* noisy top. People are looking.

P Day + 239

There's a load of polystyrene bits flying around my balcony. Either some silly bugger has left a box outside in the wind or snow's not what it used to be.

For a small family we have so many traditions at Christmas time.

9:00 everyone's awake and excited, especially Dad who yells *Has he been* (Santa) to which we all reply *He's been.*

10:30 we sit at the end of our parents' bed and open our stockings (yes as almost grown-ups we still do this).

11:00 Mum heats up her amazing Christmas breakfast muffins and we scoff them down as if there's not a 15lb bird destined for our stomachs later.

11:30 Dad disappears to do his ablutions, leaving everyone else sat round the tree like excited children waiting eagerly for him to hurry the hell up.

12:00 Dad reappears and dishes out the gifts one by one in his comedy turkey hat, pretending that the packages are for people that they're not, lingering for a second in reach of their outstretched arm and then whipping it away into the hands of its intended. There's a 15 minute pause at some point as family friends pop in to wish us Merry Christmas on their way to lunch.

14:00 Smoked salmon sandwiches and cakes are wolfed down; opening gifts is hungry work.

15:00 This is the time for napping, watching *The Snowman/ Polar Express*/the *Only Fools and Horses* Christmas special or picking at Quality Streets. As little kids when we had new toys this was usually the time window in which we realised we had no batteries.

19:00 Everyone goes to get changed for dinner, a sparkly top maybe and a quick wipe around the face to get rid of nap drool.

20:00 Dad bagpipes in the turkey. Yup you read that correctly. My northern English father Irish bagpipes the turkey into the dining room playing *Scotland the Brave*. This will make sense to anyone who's ever met my dad. For anyone else we'll just gloss over it, it'll only, like the piping, make your head hurt.

23:00 I have a bit of a walk around the house to digest while everyone settles down to watch TV/nap.

24:00 Indigestion kicks in and everyone heads to bed.

It's perfection. Our parents do the festive period so well that my brother and I struggle to be anywhere else, it never feels quite right, but we're getting to that age where we need to see our boyfriend's/girlfriend's family too. This year my brother is in Malaysia visiting the in-laws so it's just me, Mum and Dad. Three of us feels too small to stick with what we normally do so I, as a throwaway comment, suggest that they come to my flat and spend Christmas there; we'll make some different traditions.

And they took me up on it. I don't think they've realised that this means instead of Mum's culinary prowess they've got me winging it this year. But I'm excited. I thought it would be years, a husband and two kids before I'd feel grown up enough to host Christmas but here I am with none of those boiling a gammon in Coke like a pro. It means so much in a year of big challenges that I can have my family in my house, eating my food, drinking my wine from my gold stemmed bejewelled glasses (obvs) at the end of it. We've come a long way together.

London Christmas traditions. Walk. Pub. Skype. Turkey crown. Family. And it's glorious.

P Day + 242

Oh how things have changed.

I went out to the sales this morning and came back with tiles, paint, brushes, storage boxes and coat hangers to tart the flat up a bit. I then hit the online reductions and treated myself to a long handled microfibre cleaning cloth for doing my windows. All over London there are shoes crying because I haven't taken them home.

I seem to have lost the ability to nap or sleep past 8:30am over the past year. I've always been one of life's great sleepers, I think I take after my great-grandad who successfully slept through part of World War Two. But recently I'm bolt upright in bed before my alarm goes off and my beautifully soft, nap shaped sofa gets barely more than a slouch most days.

I'm not sure at what point things went wrong. It could be that living in a new flat means there are always chores to be done and sleep feels wasteful. Or that getting up early to wait for furniture deliveries that promise a window of 7am-9pm but never arrive have got me into a pattern. Or that the past year's adventures have left me in a state of cat-like readiness that doesn't spell lie in.

People tell me that Parkinson's makes you tired, that your body craves rest, that the medications make you drowsy. And yet I'm still awake. I've tried hot chocolate before bed. Eye masks to block out the annoying sliver of light that snakes down the side of the blinds every morning. New pyjamas and snuggly napping attire. Homeopathic sprays/drops/tablets/bath oils. Early nights. Late nights. But without fail I'm awake at 8:30 on a weekend.

My parents being here for Christmas seems to have broken the pattern though, somehow. I'm napping during the day with all the smugness of a benefits cheat. I could easily sleep through a whole day if no one woke me. I can't help but think it might be because there are grown-ups here. However well I think I can hold it together, play house and at being an adult the presence of genuine real grown-ups takes the pressure off, there's people to share the responsibility of potential house emergencies with, I can stop freaking out about falling in the shower and no one finding me until I get eaten by stray dogs and the neighbours notice the smell.

The downside to my new found sleepiness is I don't get up on time to change my medication patch on schedule so when I get up I'm sluggish and wobbly, but at Christmas when everyone's full of turkey and ginger wine who's going to notice the difference?

There's a new activity I'll be adding to my *not to be done while drunk* list. Right below *driving* and *shopping* now sits *take passport photos*.

I would have waited until I wasn't drunk but I'm on a bit of a deadline for this, it expires terrifyingly soon. So I plonk myself down, close the curtain and try to wind the little stool to the right height without making myself vomit. Why is the light in these booths so unflattering? Surely making the entire country look like heroin dependant axe murderers isn't beneficial to our status overseas; making us all look like supermodels with glowing skin might boost our tourist industry no end.

I manage to sit still and not smile for one of the four photos it takes so I select that and wait for what feels like a year for it to be printed. And when it comes out it seems to have been replaced with a photo of a member of the undead, a zombie must have slipped in after me. On closer inspection – no, it's me. Back inside we go. What this face needs is some colour. So I grab my make-up bag and using the screen as a mirror slap on lipstick, blusher and concealer for the eye bags. So much better. No. No. No. Yes that one will do. Long wait outside.

Oh so now I'm a Drag Queen. Jolly good. It seems to have applied its own make-up to my face during the printing process. And I have no more coins so it's a choice between zombie and Drag Queen. Zombie. Drag Queen. Zombie. Drag Queen.

I plump for zombie. It's worryingly the one that looks most like me.

P Day + 245

I had the weirdest dreams last night. Without the aid of cheese. Maybe it's because I'm now made up of 99 per cent Stilton.

They say the hardest times are milestones. Things like birthdays, Christmases, anniversaries of diagnosis, years passing and symptoms getting worse, more challenges being added to the list. New Year can be hard enough, I know a lot of people who hate it, the pressure of doing something fun and the assumption that you'll make big changes this year/life will be better/all your dreams will come true. One day it's one year, the next day it's a different year, and there's a party in the middle, that's pretty much it.

I love New Year, I've had some absolute stonkers in my time, mainly because I never put too much pressure on it, I just treat it like any other night out.

Top five New Years' eves:

1)   When we were younger (but old enough to babysit) my parents and Lucy's parents went out and left us in charge of our brothers. I ate an entire pipe of Pringles, got giddy on lemonade and we got caught watching *Carry On* movies when our parents came home. We felt so naughty, there were boobs.

2)   Kevin and I and a bunch of our friends went to a Narnia themed bash at a gay club. We went all out on our costumes, the club had been decorated to perfection and a small camp fawn followed me round all night.

3) When I was a student I worked in a small bar/music venue. The owners wanted us to look like we were having fun so they let us drink on New Year shifts. It was carnage. My glasses of wine for customers became more generous, I was recommending horrible shot combinations and my colleague went to change the Guinness barrel and left the tap on so when we returned the bar area was flooded with sticky black liquid and foam. It was hilarious at the time but not fun to clean up at 4am.

4) On the Millennium New Year we got dolled up and had fireworks in the back garden. That was the first time I owned a proper ball gown and I felt so grown up.

5) This year we had plans to go out locally with some friends but as 12 looms closer me and the boy start feeling really ill. We've got all dressed up but by 11:45 we're in our sweatpants and t-shirts, destined to the fact we'll be watching Big Ben on the TV this year. But it's our first New Year together and it's perfect. If you ignore the sick.

New Year isn't about marking the things that are changing beyond our control. It's about pride in what we've achieved and who we've achieved it with. Siblings, friends, colleagues, family, partners in crime, they're who make New Year.

P Day + 247

Ugh.

It's the first day back at work after Christmas and I have barely anything to do. So little in fact that I'm writing this so I guess this entry is sponsored by them, thanks guys.

There's not many people in the office and the few of us that are here are clinging together with the sort of terrified camaraderie that's normally only witnessed on sinking ships, plane crashes and work away days. We've made a New Year office playlist. Opened and closed a few files. Read and binned some emails. And now I feel about ready to go home.

It's 10:03am.

I have that horrible mix of impending gloom and slight misguided hopefulness that only January can bring, I'm not normally a big worrier about what the coming year will bring but since last year dumped a huge steaming turd on me as early as April I feel like I should be on my guard.

I feel tired. I hate the fact that any holiday I book from now on will come out of my allotted 25 days. I hate that I didn't sleep well last night thus undoing all the hard work I put into napping over the festive period. I hate that I now have to try and fake enthusiasm about a New Year resolution I'll never keep. I'm basically a ball of grump. I'm the cat you don't tickle. I'm the dragon you don't poke.

I'm pretty unimpressed with myself for starting a new year with what is, quite frankly, a shocking attitude problem. Sort it out Lawton.

Ten out of ten to the man in the Post Office who managed to not laugh when I handed over my new passport photos. They really are bleak.

My old one was taken when I was 20 and you were allowed to smile in ID photography. The guy has to look at them side by side to check I'm the same person and points out that at 20 I looked a lot happier than I do in the one taken at 30. Now I know this is because now you're banned from showing any sort of personality or emotion in them, you even have to show your ears, but I can't help but think I look a little tireder, my skin more sallow, my general demeanour a bit slumpy. I'm even considering Photoshopping my eyes because, and, I've never noticed this before, my right eye is slightly sleepy looking. The toll that this year has had on my body and my emotions is showing in my face, I look grey and droopy. Photo booths are renowned for their evil lighting and unflattering angle but I seemed to somehow manage to blast through that at 20 and retain a little bit of youthful glow and sparkle.

The guy asks me *If you could, would you go back to being 20?* and I immediately answer *No* because not for any money would I go back to that period of my life when I hadn't sussed out who I was yet, everything was up in the air, I was full of angst and uncertainty, I hadn't discovered hair straighteners or tweezers, I had a fringe for god's sake. I guess sometimes I'm a little angsty now, but as a 30 year old I'm firmly rooted in who I am and what I stand for, what I want and what I won't put up with, what makes me feel good, what I can offer other people. I hear there are people with Parkinson's who are 18, I can't imagine what this feels like being at an age where life is changing and your body isn't helping out.

This passport will last me through till I'm 40. I can't help but think I'll look back at my 30 photo then and wish I'd had a better picture done while I still could. I have no idea what state I'll be in come 40.

P Day + 250

I'm feeling sick all the time at the minute. For any girl this is terrifying, Google *Persistent nausea* and get off down Mothercare sharpish if the answers are to be believed. I know it's the medication causing it but there's always a second where the doubt creeps in.

And this starts a whole spiral in my head of how I feel about having children and when to do it. Sensible me says I should get cracking as soon as possible because it's only going to get harder for my body, but I know that's not the right reason to have children. I've always believed you should get to a point where you don't mind your life being turned upside down, where you've done all your being selfish, where you've had a decent time as a couple just the two of you and then you're ready to bring a small person into the world to join your gang.

According to my friends with children this is ridiculous. Apparently there's never a good time in your life to have a child, there'll always be a reason you're not ready; jobs, money, living situations, family dramas etc and even when you want to get pregnant it's not as easy as wanting it and it happens. People try for years with no success.

I've just bought a small one bedroomed flat with lots of sharp corners by a large unmanned area of water. It's not the right time. But one day I guess it will be.

P Day + 261

There was always a danger in adding super nurse as a friend on Facebook. She now knows I'm doing too much fun and not enough sleeping rather than just guessing at it by the bags under my eyes.

I've been noticing recently that I'm getting more and more impatient. If I get something in my head I have to do it now. NOW now not in five minutes now. Not after I've finished the other task I'm halfway through now. It's getting really annoying. It means I have half completed jobs all around the flat; DIY I'll never finish, clothes that need fixing that only made it out of the wardrobe and into a pile, book chapters I start and then...

Ha! Only teasing.

Tonight we're having a house warming party, everyone's due at seven and at five rather than the cleaning I'm supposed to be doing I've started assembling a shelving unit in our storage cupboard. Vital for a party obviously. It's where all the guests will be looking. The shelving doesn't fit so I have to saw bits off and disassemble parts of it and as I get halfway through I get bored and wander off to find something to wear at the party leaving the boy surrounded by little piles of sawdust, half assembled shelving and fragments of wood.

Ooooh I wonder if I could make a picture frame out of the extra wood. I'll grab my glue gun.

Imagine trying to get a tutu off a Buckaroo! horse and you're some of the way towards picturing the challenge that's facing me as I get undressed this morning.

This is of course the morning after last night's house warming in which it turns out I drank a pint of vodka and prosecco, was sick over my balcony onto the W of the Waitrose sign (the perfectly shaped receptacle) and put myself to bed in my party dress before my guests had left waking up only to fall out onto my very sharp very pointy bedside cabinet and inform everyone (now pointing camera phones at me) that I was ok.

From the messages I've received (digging under the jokes and banter) I think it sounds like it was a good night. I'm hastily texting round my new building mates to let them know they don't share external walls with a raging alcoholic nut job. I'm texting old friends letting them know I'm still alive. I'm texting workmates about the most recent episode of *Girls* and what I'm having for dinner because quite frankly last night's behaviour is the norm for them.

I am a shambles as far as alcohol is concerned nowadays, I drink so little of it that when I do I seem to have no shut off, rip cord or emergency eject mechanisms. When I was a drinking stalwart I never got bad hangovers, I could keep drinking for hours, I was always one of the last ones standing. Now I drink a bottle of rosé, three glasses of industrial strength punch, another two of the same punch but without the fruit juice, two glasses of prosecco and what I'm now told could well have been a pint of vodka and I'm paralytic. Pah! I've lost my touch.

My friend Richard swears that he only gets sick when he stops drinking, that his body is made of wine, and when his grape levels drop to dangerous levels that's when things go wrong. I'm inclined to agree. I never had Parkinson's when I was a heavy drinker.

I'm out of the dress finally and into the shower and it's only then it hits me I haven't changed my medication patch; the massive earthquake of a shake that's rumbling through my body and threatening to make me fall face first into my Imperial Leather suds is neat Parkinson's. This is how I'd be without the medication. I'm both terrified at how wobbly I've become and dazzled by modern medicine all in one.

I call my mum for sympathy. I get this. *Emma I can just about handle excessive drinking but what I won't abide are crimes against Waitrose.*

Better dig out my long-handled mop.

There's always something strange about returning as a customer to somewhere you worked. You spent so much of your day there, you ate there, you gossiped there, you bonded with people over a shared peev that at the time consumed you and now you can't even remember what it was. It was your second home and now it's just a building and going there you feel like a stranger.

For a while a few years ago I went freelance and set up my own design company. I loved working for myself but it didn't like me. Because I was a slacker. I'd take long lunches, run personal errands and dodge the work I had to do. I rented various offices to sit and not do work in and when desk space became available in Pink Floyd's recording studio I leapt at the chance to not work there too. My office was in the converted flat at the back of the studio, where the band stayed when they were recording, and the musical instruments and sound technicians all around me became my daily distraction. Needless to say things were fun for a bit and then the money ran out and I had to take on an evening job to fund my not working through the day. I know. I'm confused as to why I just didn't just work during the day too.

I found a job at a nearby market research facility as an assistant. I helped run focus groups, recorded audio and video, acted as concierge and waitress to the clients and kept the reception ticking over. It was hard work but I loved it. I made some solid friendships over the late nights and it was a very important place to me for a couple of years until the penny finally dropped and I got a proper day job instead. But I believe in leaving doors metaphorically open and always thought I might be back some day.

Tonight I'm returning as a customer. I've been asked to take part in a focus group and as I walk through reception I feel a mix of emotions. It's a very different feeling from the usual pathos you get on returning somewhere, I feel awkward and exposed. And I realise why. There's still people I know behind the desk and the place is still the same, but I'm different. I couldn't do the job any more, my hands couldn't press the record button, I'd shake as I took a tray of food in, my writing on forms would be too scrawly to read.

For someone who always likes to leave doors open, it's hard when one slams.

I hold my tension in my shoulders and the last year feels like a scarf made of stone. So I'm treating myself to a massage.

I love spas. I'm so easily calmed by the smell of geranium oil or the tinkling melody of a relaxation CD that I think I probably should be a hippie. When I was younger I had reflexology every week to build up my immune system. A lady put me in a garden chair with a blanket over me while she massaged pressure points on my feet and every week I fell asleep and she had to wake me up so I could go home and she could have her dinner. They were some of the best sleeps I've ever had.

My therapist today has the soothing voice and calming environment down pat. I'm aware that I'm shaking so I P bomb her. And as she starts to massage my shoulders I feel something change in me. I'm still. I'm not shaking. It feels strange but amazing. And as she moves to my back I'm like jelly, not tight and rigid. I feel a bit like crying. Good tears.

I wonder if you can get massages on the NHS?

According to my hairdresser it's been over a year since I had a cut. I can believe that. Recently I've been more mop than person, bedraggled and unkempt.

As a rule I don't like having my hair cut and it costs a fortune so I try to put it off for as long as I can, giving in only when it's so straggly and tangled that running a brush through it feels like I'm trying to get classified information out of myself. And when me and my wallet do finally relent I only allow one particular person near it. He's a wizard with scissors and more importantly makes conversation with you like he cares rather than the traditional forced chat about holidays and work.

I have to P bomb him. And the man on the reception desk. And the lad who washed my hair. All in quick succession. Triple whammy.

Since I was diagnosed I've been lucky to have a fair few other people with Parkinson's get in touch and offer me advice or an ear to moan to. A few of them I talk to online regularly because it helps to speak to someone who knows what you're going through. But I'm yet to meet any of them in person.

Tonight I'm supposed to be going to a group, where younger people with Parkinson's can meet up and chat. I swear I planned on going, I thought it might be fun. But as the day progresses and it's been crawling closer I've realised that I'm scared. The idea of seeing people who are a few years down the line progression wise is a terrifying glimpse into the future that I'm just not ready for yet. I also don't know how I feel about socialising with people just because they have the same condition as me. I'm sure they're all lovely with their own stuff going on in their lives other than Parkies but it goes against everything I believe in to categorise myself that way. I joke with my colleagues that some days I don't have Parkinson's. It's not that it disappears, that would be magic, but there are days when I can't be bothered to think or talk about it so I pretend I don't have it.

I'm relieved when I have too much work on to go to the group. I promise them I'll go to the next one. I might. It depends whether I have Parkinson's that day.

P Day + 278

I clap like a seal. Parkinson's has robbed me of being able to bash my hands together like a normal person, I do this weird stiff clap that looks like I'm being sarcastic. And I'm discovering this sat second row at a comedy show, not the place to show any quirks or stand out. If I don't clap I'll be singled out as rude. If I do I'm the human seal. I'm so concerned I feel like I haven't breathed for an hour. *Breathe* you idiot. The last thing you want is to faint. They're bound to notice that.

P Day + 280

I see an old friend I haven't seen for a while and she says I look 'less frail'.

Is she calling me fat?

P Day + 284

When I was younger and wanted to be an actress I'd have done anything to get into a drama school. Turns out all I really needed to do was design a website for them. We're working on a site for a well known performing arts school and I'm in the inner sanctum, the staff room, having a meeting about it. The thespian in me is massively distracted by the portraits on the walls of esteemed alumni. This is so cool.

We head out to speak to some students and then pop for some lunch before our focus groups later. As we sit in the old man's pub down the road I can feel my adrenaline levels rising, we haven't even taken a mouthful of our food yet and my stomach's all over the place. And I get that familiar homing sensation, like by whatever means I have to take I need to get home.

So I leave my colleague with a baffled face, a focus group to run all by himself and an untouched plate of chicken goujons.

P Day + 286

We're heading off to Sofia in Bulgaria where my brilliant friends Dot and Gray live. I've been out there plenty of times to visit them and I love the place but this trip is extra special, I'm a bridesmaid at her upcoming wedding and this is a planning visit.

It's a short flight, about three hours, but it's still enough to make me twitchy, I hate flying. Absolutely loathe it. It's a mix of being so high up, the turbulence and cramped seats. I never sleep, always sat in a state of cat-like readiness in case the pilot gets into trouble and needs someone to step in. Me with absolutely no aeronautical ability or credentials.

We board the plane and the weather's turned sub-optimum (I like to fly in clear cloudless skies only). The captain announces that we'll be held on the runway for a bit as there's a nasty storm to the left of us and he wants it to go away. We eventually start our race along the runway, me in my usual stance, teeth gritted, fingers crossed, feet shoulder width apart, and as we leave the ground it doesn't feel right. We're just off the ground and there's turbulence, the worst I've ever felt, and an eerie silence washes over the cabin. And then there's a huge flash just by the left wing and the plane lunges, good work captain, you've steered us right into the storm. There's talk of us being hit by lightning but the plane carries on in its ascent, we clear the storm and everything feels ok again. I loosen my grip on the boy's forearm.

For a while. Until we've been flying for an hour and are over France. Until three words come out of the captain's mouth and over the speaker that you never want to hear at 35,000 feet. *Bad. News. Folks.* We'd been hit by lightning. Somewhere around the wing engine area there might be a hole. No biggie. We were just going to have to land in Paris. I resume the stance and we land, somewhat bumpily, at Orly.

We're sat on the plane for hours while they inspect it and discover that yes, in fact, we had been flying with a hole in us, and that we'd be moved across to another, more intact aircraft for the remainder of the journey. *Facile non? Non.*

The French officers, scathing of our haphazard English security systems (the full body searches, tiny bottles of liquids, shoes off, everything scanned process) are too lax and we have to leave the plane, walk through arrivals, into departures, be security screened again, and all this at midnight. There's babies and parents having meltdowns, people wandering off the wrong way, it's not easing my anxiety levels. I'm feeling really Mr T about the whole thing if I'm honest. The massive *Sortie* sign hangs like a beacon of temptation. *Let's go to Paris instead* screams heart. *We're miles away, this is Orly, we'd have to get a taxi and a hotel and Dot and Gray would be disappointed plus our return ticket is from Sofia* goes head. Heads a boring fucker but he has a point.

So we queue up and we re-board and the whole joyous experience starts again. And I resume the stance.

Dot better appreciate this.

Gray works for the Foreign Office and the Ambassador and his wife are letting them use their residence for the wedding. It's spectacular, like a little oasis of Britishness in the centre of a bustling ex soviet city.

The Ambassador's wife welcomes us in like we're long lost friends and although the residence is old English and plush, the scattering of children's toys on the antique rug and the candid family photos perched on the grand piano make it homely. She offers us a cuppa and not wanting to be rude or cause a fuss I accept a caff one. We take them and sit in the grand room the wedding reception will be held in, all the time the fear growing that I'll spill some on the rug or leave a ring on the expensive looking table. The boy is sipping at his glass of Coke like it's champers. And what's not helping is the massive portrait of the Queen facing us from the wall behind Dot's head, watching our every slurp.

I finish without incident and as I put my cup down in its little saucer two things rise up in me. One is a familiar sensation. The second is a memory that I've already had a tiramisu and a Baileys coffee this morning. That's far too much caffeine.

Don't be sick. Not in front of her maj.

P Day + 290

Sometimes it's great pretending to be an adult. But when you return from holiday and your mum and dad have done all your little niggling DIY jobs and cleaned your flat from top to bottom, well then I'm more than happy to be someone's child.

I've had to start using rubbish fibre tipped eyeliner instead of the inky stuff because having to clean off and redo your eye make-up four times makes you very late for work and isn't a legit excuse. Apparently.

P Day + 302

The right side of my body wasn't co-operating this morning.
I'm seriously considering cutting it off if my left side could
be trusted with a knife.

I think it's safe to say I'm definitely sensitive to caffeine.

I've always thought I might be. When I was a student I had a small coffee and ended up in bed with palpitations for the rest of the day. I remember it vividly and have stayed off the devil's brew ever since. Except the odd occasion when I slip up or don't realise.

Like today. When the barista made my mocha with caff and I clearly asked for de. I felt ok for about an hour then that familiar heat started to rise in me, my stomach like a tumble dryer, my heart like a drum. And the instant desire to leg it, god knows where, but to somewhere that has a flat surface to pass out on.

And that's me done for the day. Game over. Finito. The thing that peps everyone normal in the world up is my undoing. Typical.

P Day + 306

I'm holding afternoon tea for a bunch of friends at the flat today. A sensible activity for someone who's just discovered they might be allergic to caffeine.

My brother and I have both bought houses within a few months of each other so my parents' stress levels must be through the roof. He and his girlfriend are visiting my flat for the first time today. I'm excited to show them around, take them to a pub and cook them a roast.

When we get together talk normally turns to my brother's hangovers, my job, my hangovers, his job, the usual. But this time it's like we've become adults overnight. Topics of conversation this evening have been tiled flooring, paint samples and B&Q.

My friend Sarah, who I borrowed a few years ago from an ex and who I refuse to give back, is staying for the weekend. She's starting up her own company teaching sewing classes and I'm going to be her guinea pig student. I have a little sewing machine which is a good start, and a bag of brightly coloured fabrics. She shows me how to sew a make-up bag and I'm so proud. It looks so professional.

And it starts the little cogs in my head whirring. This is something I could do more often, I've made something that looks great and the shakes didn't hinder me. I've got some plain cotton and some paints and it might be fun to make some patterned fabric and make bags from that. I could take orders from family and friends and maybe start a little business. I've got a knot of excitement in my stomach that makes me think I'm onto something.

I take Sarah out for dinner. She's helped me get my sparkle back, it's the least I can do.

We have a picnic in the park today. Looks like every other bastard had the same idea. It cracks me up how when the sun comes out London flocks to grass in the same way that ducks always find a puddle. There'll be a bit of extra rain, the field will flood and suddenly there'll be ten ducks on it like it's always been there. They must have inbuilt sensors. It's the same for humans and grass. Any grass. When the sun comes out I'm surprised you don't see people perched on central reservations and roundabouts.

And the food you fancy changes when it's sunny. Suddenly only a tiny pork pie or mini sausage will do. Like our stomachs suddenly can't handle full sized food because it's too busy sunbathing.

And the dogs. There's always a dog that wants in on your picnic, its tiny feet trampling all your cakes and it's drool soaking your sandwiches. Dogs are awesome but not in a miniature food environment. Then they're just stressful.

As you can probably tell I'm not a summer person. Mum is, she'd be bare foot all the time if she could and permanently has a healthy glow. My dad is a sun worshipper. How they spawned me and my equally transparent brother is beyond me. Give us winter any day. We stand out less.

P Day + 320

I've got that warm fuzzy feeling because I have friends round for dinner, the flat's feeling cozy and my sausage cassoulet doesn't seem to have poisoned them (unless the feeling I'm getting in my tummy isn't in fact pride but salmonella). If this is what being a grown-up is all about I might almost be a convert.

I've been beavering away since Sarah visited, painting fabric and sewing bags. I've got orders flooding in from friends and family and today I launch my online store.

I'm following in my parents' footsteps. When I was little, Mum made stuffed toys and Dad made chess sets and they'd sell them at craft fairs and to friends for extra money. It's what we do, when the chips are down we whittle them into ornaments. It feels, for the first time, like I'm taking control of my future, just a little bit and making a plan. By setting this up now it means I can grow it, steadily, and then when my real job becomes too stressful and too draining I can retire into something I love. It'll feel like a treat rather than a negative milestone. And I'm so excited.

One of the things I find most fun about having Parkies is how much it messes with your internal thermostat. I could count on one hand the amount of times I've been a comfortable temperature in the last year. Sometimes when I get really overheated I get crazy adrenaline rushes which make me feel like I'm going to pass out and sometimes I'm so cold I can't move.

Tonight I've gone to see a friend's boyfriend in an amateur performance of *Avenue Q*. I LOVE THIS PLAY. There's puppets. And they sing. What's not to like? I'm so engrossed that I don't even notice the heat starting to rise through me, from my toes all the way up to my forehead until suddenly... It's really warm in here. Is anyone else really warm? Just me? Are you sure? It's really really hot. Like uncomfortably hot. Like I feel like I might be sick all over the woman in the row in front hot. Like... oh god... I think I'm going to pass out, when's the interval? I'm looking back to see whether I could run to the door but it seems really far and if I faint then I'll be so embarrassed. *You can do this. Focus on the singing human made of felt. Breathe deeply. Smile at your friend. Everything's ok. It'll be the interval soon.*

And it comes. And I casually walk to the door like I haven't been dreaming about this moment for 15 minutes. And I excuse myself and pop outside. I breathe in the air, calm myself, take a swig of my gin and tonic and instantly I'm the right temperature, it's like it never happened.

Seriously. I've gone from feeling like I'm dying a bit to completely normal in two minutes. I was ready to call myself an ambulance it felt that serious. How is that possible? How is this fair? And how am I going to deal with this? Answers: that's Parkinson's. It's never fair. And we'll deal with the last one another time, that massive ball of fake fur is singing and I'm a sucker for fluff.

P Day + 340

I reaaaalllyy love you guyssss I do no I do and I don't say it eeenuff shush shush let me speak you're like my famly hic oops sorry sorry shhhh why are we all still here it's like reeelllly a lot later than I was thinking and this is where we wurrrrk hahahahhhhhgggg... shhh no don't don't come on that's my deshk... Why's there gin on my deshk oh it's mine hehehehe shush shush... I WANT RIHANNNNNNA PLAY RIHANNNA NEXT ooooh I want crisps can we do we have crisps... make me feel like I'm the only girl nnnnnnn ttha wwwwwwrrrlll. I'm just gna lie here for a bit.

S'ok s'ok I'm not sleepin... huuuuuhhhhhhhmake me feel like yuurrrrrr... Did I say I love you guyshhh... I do. Beeeccoz no let me say it... GIN PLEASE... because you make me schtilll feel like me...

P Day + 346

In my line of work there's a lot of last minute panics. Probably not as many as your average ambulance paramedic but they're pretty regular. Every time we pitch for a piece of work we create a beautiful document to give to the client and however early we start we always end up battling to get it finished by the time the courier comes to take it.

Parkinson's is not the slightest bit helpful when you need to do something in a hurry. If you want to know what it's like coat your fingers in butter and do whatever task you need to complete whilst doing jazz hands. The term all fingers and thumbs just about covers it. The more panicked I get the more dithery my hand becomes so I get stuck in a cycle until I have to give up and get someone else to help.

The courier is due in ten minutes and I have four docs to bind, a ribbon to tie around them into a bow and brown paper to wrap them in. I've given my left hand the responsibility of doing most of this as right hand can't be trusted. Right hand tears things, presses buttons before it's time and tends to get in the way. The courier arrives and stands and watches me and my panic gets worse and worse to the point I have to get someone else to wrap the package for me.

Let's just hope I'm never in a life or death ribbon-tying scenario.

P Day + 349

I knew my balcony would come in useful for something other than killing plants on. Today it's the London Marathon and the route takes the runners right past my flat. It's satisfying watching other people running, exhausted and sweaty, while I stand with a cup of tea and a bacon sarnie. They look like tiny brightly coloured ants from up here, scurrying in the same direction, sometimes in small packs, other times more spread out.

I've never been any good at running. At school we did this thing called a bleep test where you had to run between cones and a beep sound sets the pace of when you should reach each one. I was always behind the beep, and I could taste blood. I don't know much about sports but I don't think that's good. I did cross country for a bit and achieved very little other than the ability to wee in bushes. At sports day I was never trusted to represent my team in anything more athletic than the egg and spoon race. Last year I ran for five mins before I was beetroot red, spluttering, as out of breath as a 50 a day smoker and the sweat rings under my arms were starting to join up.

I'd love to be good at it. I watch other people pounding the pavement and it looks rhythmic and therapeutic. Plus it would be a great excuse to buy some new trainers.

P Day + 360

Finding the words to describe how I feel about having Parkinson's has come easily. I opened my mouth and they were there waiting. So when I was asked to speak to a room full of nurses and consultants about my experience I jumped at the chance. *It'll be fun* goes heart. *We know all about this* says head. We're in.

Now stood here with my crumpled notes in my tremoring hand beating out a nervous but syncopated beat on the lectern I realise I've grossly misjudged this.

Have you ever got a camera as a gift and mucked around with it for a bit, tinkered with the settings, got it working and then as the now expert on all things photography relegated the instruction pamphlet to the drawer with the dead pens and old pay slips. And you carry on using ten per cent of its potential knowing that it can do way more than just Auto, but Auto is safe, you know where you stand with Auto. That camera is my Parkinson's, I know what I know but I definitely threw the users guide away and have been getting by on the basics. Now imagine you have to stand up in front of a room full of camera manufacturers and engineers and boffins. And you're telling them all the great stuff you know about how to switch it on and how this little grey button makes the thingy click. And they're sat there knowing it has a standard ISO range of 100-12,800 and built-in NFC. That's my audience. They know more than I ever will. And that's not hard because I know zilch. Diddly squat. Nada.

I've always had an inferiority complex when it comes to presenting to people and having Parkinson's doesn't help that. Going into a room shaking makes it look like you don't know what you're doing. But I realise about half the way through my slide deck that none of these nurses are looking at my shaking hand, that not one of the consultants is focusing on the lack of confidence in my voice, they're engrossed, lapping up every word like it's the first time they're hearing it.

As I step down from the lectern my speech therapist whoops at me. And my heart and my head are proud.

When your friends get up early on a Sunday, don tutus and bright blue vests and then run through mud and climb fences and dive into dirty puddles and they do this for you, to raise money for your condition, then that's love.

When people you haven't seen in years send you a message to tell you that they're proud of you, then that's love.

When someone you've never met reaches out to say your story helped them, then that's love.

When your work colleagues take the mickey when you laugh too hard and spill your beer, then that's love.

When your brother furrows his brow when he sees you shake, then that's love.

When your parents put a hand on your shoulder and guide you through the worst of times, then that's love.

When a boy says he'll help you write your story if one day it gets too hard, then that's love.

My life is one big love story.

I'm lucky.

P Day + 365

It was exactly a year ago that I was diagnosed. A whole year since I heard the word Parkinson's and felt relief. Three hundred and sixty-four days since we left the hospital building dumbfounded but defiant, sat in a café and worked out how we felt about it. Eight thousand seven hundred and forty-two hours since we made a decision to fight the negativity that could have crept in, to enjoy our day and celebrate being together. Five hundred and twenty-four thousand and six hundred and forty minutes since we were walking by the Thames, laughing, joking, showing little p how little he meant. And thirty-one million four hundred and seventy-eight thousand and four hundred seconds later I still feel the same.

Before diagnosis I was drifting a bit, comfortable in my job, happy with my lot, I'd come through the angsty teenage years and was thinking *now what?* I was going out too much, working too late and generally burning the flaming sambuca at both ends. I looked at my friends getting hitched and having babies and didn't feel ready. So I floated. Plodded along. I think I was waiting for something to happen. And boy did it happen, just not in a way I ever would have expected.

My time before being diagnosed with Parkinson's feels like another life and another me. I think everyone at some time or another has their pivot point, that moment where something significant happens and everything shifts. My mum, my emotional compass, tells me everything in her life came together and she felt whole when she had me and my brother. That until then she felt like she wasn't completely fulfilled. I feel the same way about the change in myself since diagnosis. And this may come as a surprise – hell I may even get lynched for saying it – but I like myself a lot more than I ever have before. Parkinson's brings out a nice colour in me. I suit Parkinson's.

Being lumped with something this big puts everything into perspective, sorts the stuff you should sweat and the stuff you can shelve and makes you decisive about what you want so you push yourself to do more. It also flashes a huge light on the people who will always be there for you and ushers the fair weather friends out of the way.

Having Parkinson's is hard. Physically and emotionally. But every single cloud it brings has a diamanté encrusted lining if you look for it. Sometimes you have to look pretty hard but it's always there, and finding it fills your heart up.

I have a good excuse to buy a lot of trainers. I think I probably have more trainers than Kanye. However, I'd be willing for the man himself to challenge that claim. I've never been a high heels sort of girl and Parkinson's kindly gave me an excuse to not have to be like Bambi on ice more than once or twice a year (the obligatory birthday and New Year celebrations).

Everyone's gran has it so I get to exceed people's expectations. Don't get me wrong, I'm not ageist, there are some incredible older lads and lasses giving Parkinson's a beating. But it gets a bit weird when you tell people you have it and their frame of reference is someone a good 45 years older than you. I definitely expect more from my life and from myself than I've ever done before because I don't want to be old before my time. I don't go easy on myself just because I wobble, or stick to things that feel safe because I shake.

I know how strong I am. Not meaning to sound like a Kelly Clarkson song but there's something incredibly freeing about knowing what you can and can't handle in life. I'd still kak myself if I had to jump out of a plane or walk a tightrope but at least I know I can beat a complex neurological condition and not let it ruin my life.

My parents and friends have noticed my new outlook on life and welcome it. Now, more than ever, I feel their love and support and that spurs me on because I know whatever happens they've got my back. It makes you take risks and accept new challenges because there's never a hard fall if things go wrong, they're the cushions that appear just as I tumble. But ultimately the thing that makes every day exciting and gives me a positive starting place is feeling happy in my skin and knowing who I am. And I have Parkinson's to thank for that, it pulled me up by the boot straps and gave me a direction. I wasn't ready for it but I naturally and instinctively knew how to cope with it just like my mum did her newborn baby. And like her I can't imagine a life without it there.

I'm Emma.

I have Parkinson's.

But it doesn't, and never will, have me.

Acknowledgements

This book wouldn't have been possible without the support of my amazing family and friends. Thank you for your patience, belief and for making my life something I'm excited to write about.

Special thanks to the following people for helping turn my dream into a reality:

Peter Prior, Shramik Parmar, Annie and Ned Lawton, Jamie Lawton and Katie Shoukry, Dawn May, Richard Bateman, Albert and Liz Dungate, Pete Naish and Alex Russell, Juliet May, Kev French, Olivia Chiu and Kevin Doyle, Tom Madden, Jamie Bateman, Claire Turner, Charis Beverton, Robbie Martin, Douglas Bateman, Guy Walford, Chris and Lucy Mullan, Mark Radford, Rachel Gough, Derek Campbell, Jerome Freedman, Pal Bhachu, Patrick Smith, Inna Gjylameti, Cathy Adcock, Lisa Lyons, Kristin Jansson, Rowena Jones, Victoria Talbot, Sarah Meakes, Ryan Button, Nimisha Parmar, Robyn North, Paul and Katharine Meader, Dan and Emma Baker, Rob van Tol, Charles and Deborah Montlake, Aiden Tracey, Lamija Muzurovic, Dorothy Tomalin and Graham Glen, Charlotte Lipman, Charles and Penny Tomalin, Michael Bel Gil, Miles Clark, Marcus Weddell, Amy Sansom, Luke Williams.

Emma's Army marches on.